Is God
In Your
Marriage?

By Dr. Leo & Molly Godzich

Published by NAM E
The National Association of Marriage Enhancement

THE NATIONAL ASSOCIATION OF MARRIAGE ENHANCEMENT

For more information and additional resources contact:
www.nameonline.net
or the
NAME National Headquarters
P. 0. Box 71100
Phoenix, Arizona
85050
602-404-2600
602-971-7127 fax
info@nameonline.net

Library of Congress Cataloging-in-Publication Data:
Godzich, Leo M.
Is God in your marriage: marriage...as He meant it to be / Leo Godzich
ISBN 0-9712847-0-9
1. Marriage - Religious Aspects - Christianity 2. Godzich, Leo
Printed in the United States of America

Acknowledgements

To my precious wife, *Molly*, whose unfailing love, tolerance, patience and understanding have increased my love for God as I have learned to love my wife. Thank you for the incredible mothering of our lovely, wonderful children; for always releasing me to fulfill God's call on my life; for undergirding our ministry in intercession; and for being you, His unique creation designed for this strategic time. *I love you so much!*

Special Thanks
A very special thank you to Pastor Tommy Barnett for friendship, vision, guidance and love, and for your faith in my crazy dreams. You are the best Pastor I would ever hope for or have.

Cover design by Mark Knoles, BlazingStudio.com

The many close friends and ministry workers who are always there to pick up where I leave off and whose servant's hearts reflect the heart of God who are now too numerous to mention, especially Kim Smith whose editing made sure this third printing was the best yet.

Blessings to the two special people whose desire to anonymously support this project made it a reality.

**Blessed be the Name of the Lord,
who daily loads us with benefits!
Psalms 68:19**

Contents

PART ONE
THE PURPOSE OF MARRIAGE

MARRIAGE IS NOT COMMITMENT

God did not make marriage to make you happy. God made marriage to spiritually mature you. Adam had everything men look for. Yet God created marriage so that Adam had an opportunity to mature, to procreate and to give greater glory to God.

Adam had purpose, power, dominion over all the earth, provision and the fruit of the garden. He had everything most men look for, yet God said, *"It is not good that man should be alone."* Genesis 2:18

Why would Adam, if he had a wonderful vertical relationship, where he walked with God in the cool of the evening, need more? Because God understood that our imperfect humanity would have less of a glimpse of His divine perfection if there was not a horizontal relationship in which we could both express and receive love. Through this relationship we have a greater understanding of His love for us.

The entire Bible is about marriage. It is about relationship and character, and the ultimate expression of these two elements is the marriage of Christ to His beloved bride, the church.

At the time this book was written, I'd been preaching from the Bible on marriage every Sunday for five years without repeating sermons. I was able to do this because the Bible continually deals with marriage from the establishment of marriage in Genesis to the marriage supper of the Lamb in Revelation.

Is God in Your Marriage?

What's our final destination? Revelation tells us it's the marriage supper of the Lamb. If you want to enjoy it there, you'd better start learning how to manage your earthly marriage now. Sadly, most people spend more time planning their wedding than they do their marriage.

Once married we begin to think we can coast along. And we're possessive, aren't we, men? God did not make your wife to make you happy. God made your wife to complete you and humble you.

Marriage is a humbling experience. It means being humbled by the same person day in and day out for the rest of your life. You might as well receive it and accept it; otherwise, you'll walk in the flesh and end up resenting your spouse.

Marriage is an incredible institution. It's one of the most adventurous things you can do. Being married is like being an astronaut because you are boldly going where no man has dared to go before. Yet the difference is that when an astronaut comes back there's a ticker tape parade and there's applause. But those who have a wonderful Christian marriage generally don't get recognized, at least not on earth.

Marriage Is Not Commitment

To call marriage a commitment is an offense to God. It brings the holiness of the first institution He created to the mere level of our mental determination. This book is designed to show you that God has a plan for marriage, and that God's plan works if we work God's plan. Yet, most people do not take the time or expend the effort necessary to learn what God's plan for their marriage really is.

Marriage is a blood covenant. In biblical terms, a blood covenant is defined as a promise entered into with and before God, that shall not be broken and is sealed in blood.

When a blood covenant was broken, the ensuing consequence was death. And even today, when the covenant of marriage is broken by divorce, a form of death ensues.

God created covenant relationship so that a bond of promise indi-

10

cated a right standing with Him, which would place one in a position to receive blessing, destiny and wholeness from God. God designed marriage as a covenant to bless man and to make him more spiritually mature.

Why do you think God wants to bless your marriage? It's for one sole purpose. So that He might be glorified. If the church is the bride of Christ, then each and every marriage should aspire to be the physical manifestation of the invisible reality of Christ and His bride! How good would the condition of the church be if your wife represented the church?

IF THE CHURCH IS THE BRIDE OF CHRIST, THEN EACH AND EVERY MARRIAGE SHOULD ASPIRE TO BE THE PHYSICAL MANIFESTATION OF CHRIST AND HIS BRIDE!

Ladies, how many people would be won to Jesus if your husband was the representation of the Lord Jesus Christ?

What we want to look at in marriage is our individual responsibility. A good marriage is not husband and wife coming together. The world teaches that. A good marriage is two individuals individually seeking after God. As a result, they come together, in addition to having a common spiritual foundation with which to weather the storms of life.

And the storms will come. The Bible says, "the afflictions of the righteous are many" and "all those who are godly in Christ Jesus shall suffer. "

Look at the great men of God; they suffered greatly. One grows most in life in times of conflict and trouble. A great marriage doesn't avoid conflict or the storms of life. Instead it finds a way to position itself for God's blessing despite the situation.

Conflict is good in marriage. My wife, Molly, and I like to have a good disagreement. We've learned we need to agree to disagree agreeably. We are different people.

If you don't accept the differences in your spouse, who is God's individual and unique creation, then you're going to try to change your spouse, and you can't do that. An individual will change due to the Holy Spirit of

God and their own will -- not what you do or say. You can have a part to play: your intercession, prayerfulness, lovingkindness and other character attributes all have a part, but it's not you who changes your spouse. If you don't realize that, then you won't accept them as an individual creation whom God has fearfully and wonderfully made.

That's what happened to Adam. God took woman out of his rib, not out of his heel or his backside, but out of his rib, by his side. He took woman out of his rib because that's where she should be, close to his heart.

Now why do you think it says God caused a deep sleep to fall on Adam to take one of his ribs? Have you ever tried to take "ribs" away from a guy when he was awake? Adam looked and said, "Ah, this is flesh of my flesh, bone of my bone. She shall be called Woaaah, Man!"

God made us, as men and women, to be different. That's when we begin to accept each other -- by acknowledging our differences. In fact, the greatest marriages I observe are those where people are most different.

I once said that to someone and they asked me, "What about multiracial marriages, or multicultural marriages? Don't they have difficulties?"

I said, "They can, but often they have grounds for a greater marriage." There are a lot of people who have trouble with multiracial marriages, but be careful what you say because when Miriam came against Moses' multiracial marriage God struck her with leprosy. Moses, in his mercy, fasted for seven days to ask God to heal her. Read it for yourself in Numbers chapter 12.

If you have a problem with multiracial marriages, fix your thinking or you grieve the heart of God. Sometimes those with multiracial or multicultural marriages have an advantage in their marriage because they've already learned to understand differences in thinking.

We all function within our own frame of reference. When I say the word "ruler" to one person who was good in geometry in school, he gets a warm feeling because he has a positive memory within his frame of reference concerning "ruler". But to the person who was punished by his father with a ruler, then frustration or anger or pain come into his heart. So we all deal within our own frame of reference.

This book is an effort to communicate some things to you about marriage that God has shown, so that if you deal within God's frame of reference, it will minister to you for permanent and lasting change.

But whenever we communicate, we don't know if we're really communicating, because we all deal within our own frame of reference.

Several years ago Molly and I were on the island of Maui, Hawaii, "suffering" for the Lord. Through a benefactor in the church we were driving a beautiful Mustang convertible, just tooting along on the island when I saw a sign and I said, "Oh honey, there's Wailea (leee-ah)."

And she said, "No honey, it's Wailea (lay-ah)."

1 said, "NO, it's Waileee-ah."

And she said, "NO, it's Wailay-ah."

And as our voices rose, being in marriage ministry, we thought we'd better settle it. So we pulled into the first establishment we saw, and walked up to the counter. The young man at the establishment asked what was wrong.

I said to him, "Please, sir, tell me -- very slowly -- exactly where we are."

He gave us a peculiar look and said, "B u r r - g e r K i i ing."

That didn't actually happen, but it illustrates that we all deal within our own frame of reference. You've got to get to the place where you begin to understand your spouse's frame of reference.

Men and Women Are Different

One can begin by understanding how differently God created men and women.

In 1981, Dr. Roger Sperry won a Nobel prize for his work in neurobiology where he found that the male child, in its mother's womb between the 16th and 24th week of development, undergoes a chemical bath at the brain stem, the corpus colossum. From that point on, the corpus colossum is separated and the male child only thinks with one half of his brain at a time, while the female child continues to use both halves simultaneously.

Many women think this confirms that men are born with brain damage. But God created us that way for a purpose.

Men use one half of their brain at a time (usually the left side)-- that makes men more logical -- and it makes women more relational, because they're using both halves. Often, the differences are taught highlighting that women are more emotional, but I don't believe that's true. Women are more relational because of the simultaneous use of both halves of the brain. In general, they may be more emotional, but they are in fact more relational, that is, using emotion and logic.

There are many couples where the man can be more emotional than the woman. If the woman has gone through trauma in her early childhood, she deals with her frame of reference and learns to lock out emotion. But nonetheless, she cannot deny God's creative purpose in her life, that is, she's relational. She deals with the emotional and the logical sides simultaneously which makes her relational, whereas men use primarily the logical side.

That's why men want to get from point A to point B and don't care what happens to anyone along the way.

Women want to get from point A to point B, too, but they want to know everything that happens to everybody along the way. That's the way God created us.

I can talk to my mother on the telephone for five minutes, hang up and my wife says, "So how's your mom?"

I say, "Fine."

She can talk to her mother for twenty minutes on the telephone and I dare not ask what happened in the phone call. Not only will I get the play-by-play, but I'll also get the color commentary and the post-game show. So before I know it, it can take thirty-five minutes to express what happened in the twenty minute phone call.

That's the way God created us. The beginning of understanding each other is understanding how differently God created us.

Depending which studies you adhere to, women need to speak an average of 70,000 words per day. Men, on the other hand, need to speak an average of 20,000-25,000 words per day.

What happens to a lot of men is they're at work, dealing with people in business, and inter-acting all day long. They spend their 20,000-25,000 words before they even get home. Mom is at home going goo-goo, ga-ga with her small children. When he gets home, she still has 68,942 words left. This could create a communications challenge.

Since God created us differently, we often don't understand each other. Frequently, wives want to talk when the couple lays down in bed.

The husband is thinking, "Now, I don't know about you, but I thought laying down in bed was to go to sleep. When I put my head on the pillow, I'm supposed to close my eyes and fall asleep, not discuss the important matters of our family."

Don't take your critical discussions to bed. This will usually end up being unfruitful and cause strife. Why open the door to the possibility of what the Bible warns against: *"Do not let the sun go down on your wrath, nor give place to the devil."* Ephesians 4:26,27

God has created us differently; it's evident in children. One might observe two four-year old children in the same room, a boy and a girl.

Johnny is playing with his dump truck. You might walk in the room and call out, "Johnny! Johnny!" But he continues to play. He's going to dump that load before anything else happens. He is logical and task oriented.

But you walk in the room and you don't even have to say, "Sally". She's playing with her five little dolls and her teacups and she feels you in the room. She turns around and knows you're there because she's relational.

That's why a man and a woman can walk into a party, and the husband can jump into a two-hour conversation with three guys, talk about the Phoenix Suns for the whole time and walk away thinking it was a great time.

Whereas, as soon as his wife walks into the room, she thinks and feels, "Oh, those people over there are upset and those other people seem down. Oh, there's tension over there." She feels it.

That same couple goes to their car afterwards, he opens the door for her and says, "That was a good time."

She says, "Really?"

So she wants to find out and says, "So what did you talk about?"

He says, "We talked about the Phoenix Suns."

She says, "Well, who did you talk to?"

"Uh, what's his name, the guy with the short hair." He talked to three guys for two hours and doesn't even know their names.

Meanwhile, ten minutes into the conversation, she knows three new friends' names, their children's names, ages, etc.!

God has created us so very differently. Unless we begin to accept the fact that God has created us differently, we don't have a point of reference from which to communicate with one another. God has intentionally done that by creating us differently. Marriage is being attacked today because it is foundational: the very first institution God created.

Without marriage we don't have family. Without families we don't have church, community, societal order, etc.

We have it backwards. We think we have to have a great youth program to draw the families into the church. We think we have to elect the right government officials to stop abortion. That's not God's plan at all!

God's plan is that if He is to be glorified, then it begins with me. If I get my life right, then I can get my marriage right. If my marriage is right, then I can have my family right. If my family is strong, we can help other families get strong. If we have a bunch of strong families, we'll have a strong church and if we have a bunch of strong churches, we'll change society. That's God's plan!

MARRIAGE IS UNDER ATTACK TODAY BECAUSE IT'S THE VERY FIRST INSTITUTION GOD CREATED.

God's plan is to work through the local church to change society, not through government. Government was something man instituted after God's structure of family and society had fallen apart. That was not God's plan.

Men and women are created so differently. Sometimes we let our differences annoy us and they are typically petty. Most things that will trouble you in your marriage are petty. In the Song of Solomon it says, *"Beware the little foxes that steal the grapes and spoil the vine."*

When God said in Ephesians 6 to put on the whole armor of God, the shield of faith is designed to stop the fiery darts of the enemy. Not the fiery *arrows*, it's the *darts, the little things* that will weigh you and tear you down. You've got to guard your heart against those little things that build up resentment to where you're so full of negative emotion that you can't let the positive love of God flow through you to your spouse.

That's why we have to work at marriage. We work at every other relationship in our life: our business relationships, church relationships, and our careers. But we get married and think it's just supposed to happen. That's the state of many marriages today. Why? Because it's the institution Satan attacks most.

A Battle on Three Fronts

There are at least three main reasons Satan attacks marriages.

The first reason is because Satan wants to hurt you, not so much just to hurt you, but as a means of hurting God. Hurting you is serendipity; it's a side benefit to Satan. He wants to destroy your marriage because he wants to hurt God. He knows he can't defeat God. But he knows he can grieve God.

If you beat me up that's one thing, but if you beat my children up that hurts me more. So it is with God. Satan knows he can't beat God up, but if he can beat God's children up and make them hurt in their most endearing relationship, then he knows he's grieved the heart of God.

Secondly, he wants to stop God's power. By ruining a marriage, Satan has diffused God's plan for power. Why are our churches powerless? Because our couples are powerless. Dealing with the demonic realm; *"One could chase a thousand, and two put ten thousand to flight."* Deut. 32:30 Two people agreed should walk in ten times the spiritual power.

Who better for me to be in agreement with than the gift of God, my spouse, who knows me most intimately? Who better to discern spirits with me?

The person you spend the most time with is the person you should learn to pray with and the one you should learn to do spiritual warfare with most.

The third reason Satan and the kingdom of darkness attacks marriages is to deny the development of a righteous generation. The children of divorce go through so many different stresses and pressures. These often thwart their ability to trust in God. The fatherless have a difficult time relating to the magnificent love of a Heavenly Father. Children who are taught that God can do anything, wonder how that teaching applies if their parents say, "It just can't work!"

We must understand that the principles of spiritual warfare are vital to our marriage. There is an enemy attempting to stop you from building your marriage to be all that God meant it to be!

God did not make marriage to make you happy, He made marriage to spiritually mature you, so that He could have godly offspring. He desires a righteous generation that would continue to multiply and replenish the earth and grow in the peaceable fruits of righteousness that would be light in a dark and dying world. That's why your children need to be godly. You must train your children in a godly manner.

No one really does a fine job of training their children unless they themselves are walking in love and operating in the fruit of the Spirit. Satan would relish the opportunity to use your marital relationship, what God intended for good, to imbalance you spiritually so that the Gospel would be discredited to your children.

Satan is attacking God's kingdom one family at a time. We must realize that the first battlefront in the war on families is our marriage.

If our marriage is a covenant relationship with God and with one another, then Satan has no authority in that relationship. But when we step outside the boundaries of that covenant, we open ourselves up to the influence of the god of this old world, the prince of the air and his kingdom of darkness, Satan and his evil forces.

Initially the permanence of covenant relationship may seem confining and restrictive. Upon implementation, it becomes energizing and liberating. Within a society that focuses on self, it would be perceived as counterproductive to give yourself to another for the rest of your life.

When 1 realized that my marriage was blood covenant with God, I said to Molly, "Hey, honey, you're stuck with me because I didn't just exchange vows with you, I exchanged vows with God."

The declaration of total promise to God evidenced in permanent promise to this one and only monogamous relationship, set me free. No longer was there the possibility in my mind that things "might not work out". We had declared to God that, come what may, we were going to work it out with His help.

God wants you to realize the blessing of permanence in marriage. In our role as the bride of Christ we worship God with psalms and choruses proclaiming, "There is none like You" and "You are God, there is no other." Our marriage must also reflect the fact that we've settled it in our mind and heart.

> **NO LONGER WAS THERE THE POSSIBILITY THAT THINGS "MIGHT NOT WORK OUT". WE HAD DECLARED TO GOD THAT, COME WHAT MAY, WE WERE GOING TO WORK IT OUT WITH HIS HELP.**

It's a matter of decisive intellect (determination) and willful desire (free choice) that there will be no other possibility because this is the one for me!

Newlyweds would do well to reap the benefits of a covenant mentality, even when they are just beginning to learn more about each other. Knowing that you've covenanted together forever, frees you from trying to change your spouse and allows you to enjoy the journey of discovering how different you are. We must accept and receive each other as God's gift because He knows what we need, even when we don't.

THE MYSTERY OF MOTIVATION

What motivates most people? What is this dilemma of human motivation? Why do we do the things we do? In 85% of the couples that file for divorce only one spouse wants to divorce. In less than 10% of all cases do both husband and wife want the divorce, and even then, in my opinion, most are misguided. That's remarkable! Why don't we see more marriage ministries reaching out? Why isn't the church reaching out to these couples in need? I think a lot of it has to do with a basic lack of understanding God's plan for motivation.

What motivates us? Throughout history man has pondered motivation. There are secular answers. Sigmund Freud thought sex and pleasure are our basic motivating factors. Pavlov thought it was all behavior related. He basically believed that we are victims of our environment.

To a certain extent we are victims of our environment. Just as to a certain extent Freud was right that we are motivated by sex and pleasure. But those are not the basic influences of human motivation.

Later, along came secular humanism that says we are motivated by a self-actualization. That out of ourselves, once we determine who we are, then we are motivated humanly.

All these concepts are erroneous. They're wrong. It's not God's plan for motivation. Even in the western church today and in our western culture we think that maturity and spirituality is equated with self-reliance. When someone is self-reliant or when someone is totally confident, we think that he's mature or spiritual. That's not God's plan either.

God does not want a self-reliant church, yet in a lot of Pentecostal and Charismatic circles today the idea is, "Boy if you can't find the answers for yourself, you're wrong with God! If you're not walking in total victory all the time then there's something wrong with your spirituality!"

That's simply not God's plan. In fact, God wants us to be reliant: reliant on Him and reliant on others.

Today the church in America is a lot like the church of Laodicea in Revelation 3. It says that the church was in need of nothing. The United States today has this attitude that we're in need of nothing, yet we are a very needy people. We are very dependent.

The church that's in need of nothing is lukewarm in God's mouth and He will spew it out. He'll spit it out. That's the way the American church is today because of this prevailing attitude of self-reliance. The attitude that I have everything I need and I need nothing else is in our churches today. God wants us to be a needy people and He has a plan to overcome our perceived independence.

A lot of times people run into problems because they think, "If only, if only, if only...if only I had the perfect job..."

We think, "My spouse is not perfect. If only I had the perfect spouse. If only my spouse was more spiritual. If my spouse was this way then I could really rise and have my needs met." But this attitude of seeking perfection in our spouse, our jobs and our churches is a lie. And it's a deep-seated lie.

Adam had it close to perfect. In the garden he had a perfect position. He didn't need a thing. He had everything he needed to eat. He had dominion over the animals. He had everything he needed to possess.

Sometimes people seek possessions to find fulfillment, to find that basic motivation. Adam didn't need a Mercedes. He had everything he needed to possess, because he had dominion over all. Everything that was there he possessed.

Adam also had position. A lot of times people seek fulfillment in their position in life, in recognition from others, or where they're placed in relation to other people. But Adam had that, too. The Bible says he was exalted above every living thing on the earth. He had position. He had possessions. He had perfection. He had everything he needed there.

It Was Not Good Enough

We see in Genesis 2, God's plan is not that we should be motivated by possessions or position. Genesis 2:18 explains, *"And the Lord God said, "It is not good that man should be alone; I will make him a helper comparable to him."*

It is not good that man should be alone! Adam had perfection, possession, and position. He had everything he needed, or so he thought. But God recognized he didn't have everything he needed. And He said, "It is not good that man should be alone."

Adam had a great relationship with God. Sometimes we believe if our relationship is totally right with God we need nothing else, and in a sense that's true. If our relationship is totally right with God we need nothing else.

But God had a greater plan than that. He created within us a need for relationships with meaningful others. Even if our vertical relationship, our relationship with God, is right, we still have a desire for horizontal relationship, a relationship with an-

HE CREATED WITHIN US A NEED FOR MEANINGFUL RELATIONSHIPS WITH OTHERS.

other person, a person who can be part of our life. God created us with that desire!

Even though He saw that Adam's covenant relationship with Him was right, He said, "It's not good that he should be alone." **And that's the basic dilemma of human motivation - loneliness.**

Many times we think we want more time alone. But what we really want is a solid relationship. According to Gallup Polls, 73% of Americans struggle with loneliness at some point each month.

What's wrong with that picture of loneliness? We have the secular humanistic view that if we get alone, get the toys, get everything else, then it all falls into place and we're not worried about anything else.

Although America is the most prosperous nation ever, still 73% of us struggle with loneliness. Society creates that in us. We're cocooning. We're shutting off into our cocoons. More and more people are working at home with their PCs via phone lines using modems and faxes. More and more people are finding entertainment in their VCRs and through their cable televisions, so they're not going out and having interaction with other people.

An Anti-Relationship Mentality

We're moving as a society in our Western culture away from relationships. God wants us first to have a right vertical relationship with Him and secondly He recognizes that our need for interaction is fulfilled in a proper horizontal relationship with our spouse. But our environment yells at us that we don't need anyone else, so we develop an anti-relationship mentality.

A lot of couples have grown apart in their horizontal relationship because they've swallowed the secular lie that there is fulfillment outside your meaningful relationship. There is a socially accepted lie that says either you need to be alone or you need fulfillment in careers and other possessions. It's this pervasive attitude of motivation in our society that is wrong.

We should be motivated first by an intimacy with God and second, by developing an intimacy with our spouse. That's God's plan for motivation. We're created to need an intimate relationship with God and with meaningful others.

God's plan to reveal perfection in our lives is revealed through imperfection. Adam had everything he needed in the garden. He had relationship with God. But God was not satisfied with that. He recognized it was not good for man to be alone. He recognized that Adam needed an imperfect being like he was, in order to understand his imperfect human condition.

That's what a spouse is in our lives. They are someone who is imperfect. Your spouse is imperfect. It's someone in an imperfect condition that helps you recognize perfection. Through your spouse, God's relationship to you is more greatly revealed than if you didn't have a spouse, if you were alone, or if you thought you could find perfection in possessions, status, position, or career.

God revealed in Adam that man has a basic need to relate to someone who is imperfect. Through such a relationship we would learn more about each other and therefore be able to glorify God, who is perfect, in a greater way.

All of creation speaks about our dependence. We're dependent upon other things. We are not independent or self-reliant as many like to believe. Could you go on without air or water or food? God has created us with these basic human needs. All creation cries out of our dependence, and we have the need for fellowship.

Our fellowship with God is imperfect unless we develop proper fellowship with our spouse. God said it's not good for man to be alone.

Over the history of a marriage, a couple may accumulate a lot of hurt and resentment. Then we begin to feel the relationship is so imperfect that it's not fulfilling. But the truth is that when we recognize the imperfection of our horizontal relationship, then we can look to the relationship with a perfect God and see what adjustments need to be made.

But we've got to be able to put hurt and resentment aside. When you accumulate a lot of hurt and resentment (even little things or things you've carried from childhood), the hurt and resentment is seeded there. It tells you, "I don't need anybody. People hurt me."

"I don't need anybody" is one of the grand lies that keep people from having a fulfilling relationship. They may even think, "I don't need anyone else. All I need is God."

And it's true that you need God, but God has created you with a need for someone else. It is not good that you should be alone. In Genesis 2:18 God says, *"I will"*. He makes a declaration, a Divine order of dependence. *"I will make for him."* God declares Adam will have a help meet suitable for him. God makes a declaration. That is His first declaration for fellowship.

The first declaration of any human institution is marriage. God's plan is marriage. The second declaration God makes for fellowship is family. He promises offspring. Psalm 127 says children are a heritage from the Lord. They are a reward from Him. They are part of the second level of fellowship.

Once we have a marriage relationship, we have a family relationship. Then He creates a structure for the church. It's in those three relationships we find out who God is. Through marriage, family and church, our "aloneness" is ministered to on a horizontal, human level. All three institutions are part of God's plan that we should not be alone.

In Matthew 16:18 Jesus said, *"And I also say to you, that you are Peter, and on this rock I will build My church, and the gates of Hades shall not prevail against it."*

Upon this rock, *I will.* He declares again that He will have a church and the gates of hell will not prevail against it. That's the third level of fellowship. After marriage and family comes church.

We find out who God is through our own personal relationship with Him, through the Word, through prayer and through communion with the Holy Spirit. But in order to understand relationship, God has set this divine order of marriage, family and church so we can develop relationship.

At different times of your life certain parts of each relationship will be lacking. At times, maybe your church relationship may not be the greatest. That's when you need to focus in and intensify on your marriage and family relationships.

Perhaps a spouse's fallen condition causes your marriage to not be the best at that time. You have to find that relationship in the church. You have to continue to meet that need for companionship and relationship - to give out and receive. Freely we have received from God so freely we give. Give and you shall receive. So we need to give of ourselves.

If your marital relationship is not right you need to give out in family or in church. In the same way you need to be able to receive from family and church. Never forget, however, that the first priority, if one of those areas is lacking, is to first press into God, your vertical relationship.

So without the marriage relationship where does that leave singles?

In church. Single people should be in church. Single people should have a greater church relationship than a married person. A married person should have a greater marital and family relationship.

This is God's plan to meet our relational needs. Through our relationships we can find out who He is just as we find out who He is through His Word and through prayer.

But a lot of us in church today think, "Well, I'll go to church whenever they have service but I won't have fellowship with anyone in church." So we miss part of God's plan for relationship. We're missing part of His plan for seeing who His body is.

Accountability Requires Relationship

Relationship helps keep us accountable. Relationship lets us know that if we're out of right relationship either in our marriage, family or church, we're missing a sense of responsibility. We become like a sheep straying from the flock ready for a wolf to move in and devour us.

Interestingly, if we look in verse 22 and 23 of Matthew 16, "*Then Peter took Him aside and began to rebuke Him,, saying, 'Far be it from You, Lord,. this shall not happen to You!'*

But He turned and said to Peter, 'Get behind Me, Satan! You are an offense to Me, for you are not mindful of the things of God, but the things of men.'"

What was the problem here? As soon as God had declared another role of relationship, as soon as He declared to Peter, "You are the rock and upon this rock I will build my church", the enemy attacks.

Every time you make a declaration for relationship the enemy will attack, because he comes to kill, steal and destroy. Why? Because he knows he has blown his relationship with God.

Anytime you make a declaration for relationship in your life you can be assured the enemy will come to attack. When people declare they are getting married, the enemy will come to attack. When people have children, learning how to parent will frequently come between them. And when people make a commitment to church the enemy attacks as well. In each one of these three relationships people are attacked all the time. Whenever you declare you will improve on one of these relationships you can be sure the enemy will attack. It's interesting Jesus says, *"Get behind Me, Satan."*

But then He says, *"You are an offense to Me, for you are not mindful of the things of God, but the things of men."*

The Divine order has been messed up. Peter was not looking at God's Divine order, he was looking at man's order.

What is man's order of priority? We're made up threefold. We are body, mind and spirit. But God's order of priority is spirit first, then mind, then body.

The world's order of priority is body first, then soul, then spirit. The world has reversed God's priorities, body being the least important in God's order. Spirit is most important in God's order.

That's why man walks in the flesh. He puts the emphasis on body first; on how we look and what we feel. When we're in the flesh we go by feelings because we've got God's order for relationship out of order.

THE WORLD'S ORDER OF PRIORITY IS BODY FIRST, THEN SOUL, THEN SPIRIT. THE WORLD HAS REVERSED GOD'S PRIORITIES.

We're using man's order for relationship and putting flesh first, then mind, then spirit. Interestingly, either order of priority places mind in the middle. That's why we communicate even with the world on a mind level. We communicate through our personality with the mind. The mind is the middle ground and the battleground.

Even if you have your priority on spirit first, but your spouse has body first, then your most intimate communication is out of order because you're not communicating on the same level.

A lot of couples communicate on the mind level. Some couples have great verbal communication skills; they talk about everything. But they have little communication on a spiritual level. One or the other has God's order of relationship out of order.

If spirit, mind and body is God's order, then where should we put our emphasis on personal development? On spirit. And yet how much time do we spend developing our spirit? God's plan for relationship is that we work on developing the spirit man. Our mind man can then communicate with other minds even better if we're focused on our spirit. Then our body becomes part of God's plan.

We need to take care of our bodies by eating properly, exercising, etc. But in America we often put body first, and we've got people who look so good on the outside but yet they're so broken on the inside because they've got a humanistic order of relationship. The spirit man is way down on the priority list.

We must submit to God's plan to minister to our aloneness. If we individually work on our spirit man first, then we have right relationship in marriage, family and church. We won't be hurt by being alone. We will know, according to II Corinthians 1:3-4, the comfort of Him who has comforted us that we might comfort others. That's what we're all looking for in life. We're looking for comfort and God's grace in all areas of our life.

If we have right relationship in marriage, family and church then we can be comforted by the Comforter, the Holy Spirit, and then we can comfort others and live a victorious life. That's what God wants us to have.

But we get the relationship order out of order, and spend so little time developing our spirit man -- God's first priority. As a result of neglecting our spiritual relationship with God, we don't spend enough time on our marriage relationship, which is our second priority, nor our family and church relationships. Instead, what we do is look for possessions, position and perfection, the very things that Adam had.

Those things were enough. But God said, "No, that's not enough," because Adam was still alone. He had a one- on-one covenant relationship with God. He had all his needs met. But in reality, he didn't. He still had one more need. And that need was to not be alone. That need was to have a relationship with someone like himself so that through a relationship with others, he could develop a greater relationship with God.

What about the other aspects of our lives? Is our prayer life an act of the flesh? Do you agree with your spouse and join hands as a ritual, as a rite of obligation, or do you do it to develop the spirit person, so that the two of you are becoming one?

What about your church life? Do you attend out of obligation? Or do you come with a prepared heart saying, "Lord, change me today. Do something in my life. Increase my relationship through church so that I might grow, and become more of a spirit man rather than a flesh man."

You may have faced challenges in your relationships, and you now know the challenges occurred primarily because your relationship was out of order. You had a relationship based on the flesh and not on the spirit.

God's plan works if we work God's plan

We need to put spirit first, to emphasize our own spirit person: spirit, mind and body. Then we need to work on our marital relationship. Next we work on our family relationship. Then we work on our church relatioship.

Yet many who counsel will say, "Just keep coming to church. Everything will turn out okay. That's all right. Just be faithful."

I think church is very important. I think it's vital you attend church and that you be faithful to church, but unless you're working on those other relationships and your spirit man, you're not going to receive from church what you should receive.

Unless you're working on your marital relationship, you and your spouse will not be able to discuss what you've heard in church.

God's plan works if we work God's plan.

If we're living a life where we accumulate hurts and resentments and haven't released them because our relationship with God hasn't been great at all times, we're not going to have the abundant life. If you dwell in the past, that's where you will find hurt, anger and bitterness. Those are the things of the past.

Bitterness means that someone is living in the past. Anger often deals with a hurt or unmet need from the past. It's a form of resentment and that's how anger wells up. A lot of people don't understand anger. They think anger is a reaction. Anger is usually a result of living in the past and not having dealt with hurt or resentment.

What happens in the future? In the future you're dealing with fear, anxiety and worry.

Isn't most of what we fear something that has not yet happened? It's something in the future. F.E.A.R. is False - Evidence - Appearing - Real. We usually fear something that's false evidence -- it's not of faith -- and it appears real in our life. It hasn't happened to us yet.

That's living in the future. That's where anxiety and worry come from. If you're in the future, you're often dealing with anxiety, worry and fear. If you're in the past, you tend to deal with bitterness, resentment and anger.

Where is life more abundant? Where does Jesus meet us? In the here and now. That's the key - to attempt to live in the present. Put the past behind and do not worry about tomorrow.

God's presence always exists and is always available in the present. Live in His presence today, everyday. If you live today in proper relationship, developing your spirit man then developing your marital relationship then developing your family and having a church relationship, you can live in victory! If we don't let the sun set on our anger, if we deal with the past through confession and forgiveness, then we can forgive that hurt. If we deal in the comfort of the Holy Spirit for the future, then we can avoid fears, anxieties and worries. We need to stand on God's Word that states in Jeremiah 29:11, *"For I know the thoughts that I think toward you, says the Lord, thoughts of peace and not of evil, to give you a future and a hope."*

Then we can dwell in the Truth of God's Word and live life more abundantly today.

WHY GOD HATES DIVORCE

Most of the time when someone says, "Turn to Malachi", many people assume that the preacher's message will have to do with tithing and giving. This great book of the Bible, however, reveals why God hates divorce.

"And this is the second thing you do: You cover the altar of the Lord with tears, with weeping and crying so He does not regard the offering anymore, nor receive it with good will from your hands.

Yet you say, "For what reason?"

Because the Lord has been witness between you and the wife of your youth, with whom you have dealt treacherously; Yet she is your companion and your wife by covenant.

But did He not make them one, having a remnant of the Spirit?

And why one?

He seeks godly offspring. Therefore take heed to your spirit, and let none deal treacherously with the wife of his youth.

"For the Lord God of Israel says that He hates divorce, for it covers one's garment with violence." says the Lord of hosts.

"Therefore take heed to your spirit, that you do not deal treacherously."
Malachi 2:13-16

That is a challenging passage of scripture. God says that you cover the altar of the Lord with your tears, with weeping and crying, but he does not regard the offering anymore nor receive it with goodwill from your hand.

That's a hard saying. God is speaking in this passage to a people (much like Americans) that will come to the altar with weeping and crying but yet their offering is neither received nor acceptable. And ultimately He reveals the heart of the complaint: the offering is totally unacceptable because God hates divorce and He explains that the reason He hates divorce is because He seeks godly offspring.

God seeks godly offspring and He won't have an abundance of godly offspring in a country riddled with divorce. It just does not happen. One might argue, "Well, God is greater than all things and He'll rise above that."

Yes, He will.

"If my people, which are called by my name, shall humble themselves, and pray; and seek my face, and turn from their wicked ways; then will I hear from heaven, and will forgive their sin, and will heal their land."
II Chronicles 7:14 KJV

If you question whether divorce impedes the production of godly offspring, review some of the following reports that come from various secular sources. They show the societal impact of divorce and the single parenting of our children.

1) An analysis of fifty separate studies of juvenile crime published in *The Journal of Social Problems* revealed that the prevalence of delinquency in broken homes is 15% higher than that of intact homes. In addition, there are no appreciable differences in the impact of broken homes between girls and boys or between black youths and white youths. It doesn't matter. Kids who are devastated by divorce are 15% more likely to commit crime.

2) Former U.S. Attorney General William Barr said, "If you look at the one factor that most closely correlates with crime, it's not poverty, it's not employment, it's not education, it's the absence of the father in the family."

3) In *The Journal of Family Psychology,* Dr. Nicholas Zill writes that he found the children of divorce showed "high levels of emotional distress and problem behaviors and were doubly as likely to need psychological help."

4) Children living with mom and dad receive professional help for behavior and psychological problems at half the rate of children not living with both biological parents, according to The National Center for Health Statistics.

5) Other studies show that the general health problems of children from broken homes are increased by 20-30% even when adjusting for demographic variables (such as poverty levels and food sources). Even with these adjustments, the general health problems of children are 20-30% greater when they are victims of divorce.

6) A major study conducted in the 1980s to find out what factors kept children from excelling in school found that the number one factor was family. The family factor was a greater influence than school facilities, curriculum or staff. (I personally know many couples that, as they worked on their marriage and put their marriage on biblical ground, saw their children do better in school.)

7) Researchers from Johns Hopkins and Princeton Universities found that growing up in a single-parent family had a negative effect on grade point average, school attendance and general indicators of educational attainment.

8) Other studies show that children from low-income intact families outperform students from high-income single parent homes. Children living in single parent homes are nearly twice as likely to repeat a grade as those living with both parents.

9) Almost 75% of American children living in a single parent family will experience poverty before they are eleven years old compared to less than 20% of children in two parent families.

10) Drs. Sarah McClanahan and Larry Bumpass, two of the nation's leading authorities on the social impact of single mothering, found that young white women raised in single-parent families are 164% more likely to bear children out of wedlock themselves. Moreover, if these women do marry, their marriages are 92% more likely to end in divorce.

11) Dr. James Egan, at Childrens Hospital in Washington D.C. asserts: "A dead father is a more effective father than a missing father.

That's an amazing statement. A deceased parent will still maintain a moral and authoritative presence in the home. They're talked about in a positive manner; their pictures stay on the wall. Negative behavior by a child can quickly be corrected with a statement: "Would your father approve of that?"

But if the father has abandoned the family or never was identified, the answer to that question by the child is, "Who cares?" or even worse, "Who?" That's what is happening in our society today.

We've got to understand that even when a child loses a parent to death it has a less adverse affect on that child than experiencing the breakdown of his or her parent's marriage.

God called Himself "Father" and He wants us to emulate His role as Father. But how complete can an individual's understanding of a loving father be if they've never seen one? Unless a divine intervention of understanding occurs by the power of the Holy Spirit, that child will have a distorted perspective on what and who a father is.

God's plan is for the family is to be the basis of society.

Why? Because he hates divorce, because He seeks godly offspring.

"When they are diminished and brought low through oppression, affliction and sorrow, He pours contempt on princes, and causes them to wander in the wilderness, where there is no way." Psalm 107:39, 40

There's been oppression and affliction brought on the children of America. God has placed America, which was once referred to as 'the prince of nations and the source of benevolence', in a position of begging for help. In the past more charity went out from America than from any other nation in history. Also more missionary work went out from America than any other nation in history. As America's own children have been oppressed and afflicted by the break-up of marriages, God says that He wills America to wander in the wilderness looking for its own way.

Are we wandering in the wilderness looking for our own way? Our nation is wandering in the wilderness of immorality.

In Psalm 107:41-42 God says, *"Yet He sets the poor on high, far from affliction, and makes their families like a flock. The righteous see it and rejoice, and all iniquity stops its mouth."*

When the families of God, when the people of God are set like a flock -- when they're knit together -- then other people will see it and rejoice.

In the Nomadic tribes of Israel, the Bedouins who go throughout the Sinai desert often travel very closely, but they each have their own flock of sheep. You may see a flock of sheep here and a flock of sheep there and yet another flock of sheep there; you see them all together in the panorama of the horizon. But, if a sheep moves toward another flock, almost instinctively the flock moves a little bit towards that sheep and then that sheep returns back to the flock so that the flock can follow their shepherd.

Families are like a flock and that's what God desires. God desires that if you have a strong family unit, should even one member want out of that family, that family all reaches out and moves toward that member. That member is drawn back to that love because the righteous rejoice in families that are set like a flock. That's what God intends for the people of God today.

The worldly statistics and everything around us show us how the deterioration of the family is the major ill of society, in terms of education, in terms of crime and in terms of family structure. Children are growing up with an identity crisis, wondering whose family they are part of, that is, which parent or stepparent or set of parents they belong to.

Grounds for a Revival

The good news is that's grounds for a great revival. There's a generation of fatherless children looking for a father. I believe Father God in all His mercy is sitting up there waiting to pour out His Spirit on these children. But, He's looking for a remnant, He's looking for that remnant crowd that are the righteous - that set their families like a flock so that He can pour out His Spirit. So that those children have a place to turn to when the curse is reversed. They will have models upon which to build.

Back in verse 23-28 of Psalm, chapter 107, it says: *"Those who go down to the sea in ships, who do business on great waters, they see the works of the Lord, and His wonders in the deep. For He commands and raises the stormy wind, which lifts up the waves of the sea. They mount up to the heavens, they go down again to the depths; their soul melts because of trouble. They reel to and fro, and stagger like a drunken man, and are at their wits' end. Then they cry out to the Lord in their trouble, and He brings them out of their distresses."*

Sounds like a week of counseling in my office. People who are reeling to and fro, staggering like a drunken man from being tossed about in the storms of life. They've entered into the ships, they've been taken on the waves, they've been brought to the deep, they've been brought out again and it's only at that point of trouble and distress that they then cry out to the Lord. And He brings them out of their distress. God wants to do that for people, but then they've got to set their feet on solid ground.

Verses 29-31: *"He calms the storm, so that its waves are still. Then they are glad because they are quiet; so He guides them to their desired haven. Oh, that men would give thanks to the Lord for His goodness, and for His wonderful works to the children of men!"*

That's the answer. If you want your family to be like a flock, you've got to develop that heart of thankfulness in your family. Do your children see you on bended knee giving thanks for a roof over your head? Do your children see you on bended knee giving thanks for food on your table? Do your children see you on bended knee for the fact that the family is together, even if there is strife in the family?

They need to see that. They need to have that thankfulness for the goodness of the Lord and for what He has done for the children of men. Do your children even realize that you're thankful that your family is together or do they take it for granted? Do you tell them that there are other hurting families and that your family needs to pray for those hurting families so that they, too, can develop thankfulness for a family that's together?

If you develop in your children the daily practice of thanking God for their family, then when they're tempted to stray, that thankfulness will arise and calm the storm and draw them right back into that family unit.

But it's got to begin wherever your children are now. Even if your children are grown and away, there should be times that, at the very least, by telephone you get together with them and thank God for your family. We need to develop that thankfulness so that we can see God's heart poured out on His children.

Verse 32 says, *"Let them exalt Him also in the assembly of the people, and praise Him in the company of the elders."*

The Lord developed a group we call *Exaltation!* out of the marriage ministry we oversee at Phoenix First Assembly of God. They became an anointed worship team of musicians and singers that exalted the Lord in the congregation of the people. A group of worshippers who have weathered storms to sing God's praises for what He has done.

We need to have that time of corporate praise, that time of corporate worship where God is pleased that His people are offering a sacrifice, not just with tears at the altar, but with joy abounding and gladness.

There's a balance in the Christian life. Yes, there's a time for weeping and repentance, but there's a time to step into the joy of the Lord so that you can sense His presence, so you can be renewed, so you can regain spiritual eyes, so you can further repent.

It's like a cycle. Your repentance becomes deeper in the more spiritual things of God. As you repent and identify with a nation, no longer do you just repent for your own sins. You begin to identify the sins of a nation and repent for the fatherlessness of our generation, for abortion and for racial prejudice -- for all these national sins of America.

Then you get deeper and you weep again. You come to a place where you can get in the congregation of the people and praise Him for His good works so you're energized again.

When we seek His face in holiness, we get alone with Him. We then realize how lowly we are and how great He is and it drives us to our knees in repentance. Then we use that to see a lost and dying world. We then praise the Lord and get energized so that we can witness to a hurting society. In that way we can help our fellow man and our children.

You may be reading this book in the middle of a broken family situation. Thank God!

You may say, "Thank God for what?"

Thank God that's where you are. You won't get out from where you are at unless you begin to learn the power of thanking God where you are.

YOU WON'T GET OUT FROM WHERE YOU ARE AT UNLESS YOU LEARN THE POWER OF THANKING GOD RIGHT WHERE YOU ARE.

"Rejoice always, pray without ceasing, in everything give thanks; for this is the will of God in Christ Jesus for you." I Thessalonians 5:16-18

People oftentimes say, "What is God's will? I am looking for God's will in my life." He states it right here.

"Rejoice always, pray without ceasing, in everything give thanks; for this is the will of God in Christ Jesus for you."

Rejoice always. Get in that congregation of believers that is exalting the Lord our God, who are praising Him with fullness so that you can rejoice. Then take that strength of rejoicing.

Develop A Covenant Consciousness

If we realize that the way to overcome the trends of divorce is by understanding that God hates divorce, we develop a covenant consciousness that keeps us looking to God.

Ezekiel, chapter 16:60-63:

"Nevertheless I will remember My covenant with you in the days of your youth, and I will establish an everlasting covenant with you. Then you will remember your ways and be ashamed, when you receive your older and your younger sisters; for I will give them to you for daughters, but not because of My covenant with you. And I will establish My covenant with you. Then you shall know that I am the Lord, that you may remember and be ashamed, and

40

never open your mouth anymore because of your shame, when I provide you an atonement for all you have done," says the Lord God."

God is addressing His children, the children of Israel, and He says, "I'm going to establish a new covenant with you, a covenant that will be such a covenant that you're not even going to speak about the shame that you've endured as you've been idolatrous and adulterous towards me."

We've all been idolatrous at different times in our life and God meets us as His children and says, "I will establish covenant with you, a new covenant."

Remember, covenant is a promise made before God that will not be broken and is sealed in blood. If you broke a blood covenant in the Old Testament it was punishable by death and God established marriage as a blood covenant.

That's why the ideal circumstance is a virgin marriage because of the issue of blood that happens when a woman's hymen is broken. This is a symbol of the blood covenant of God in marriage. That's what God established it for. There's no other biological reason that there should be an issue of blood, whether it be microscopic or greater, at that moment in time.

It occurs as a seal of a covenant. In fact, your marriage is not consummated until you have relations with your spouse. Today in all fifty states of the United States, if a couple gets married and they never consummate their relationship in a physical way, then that marriage can he nullified - it can be annulled.

It's amazing that the law even recognizes God's principle of blood covenant.

God says to His children, "Wait a minute, forget the old covenant. You've already broken that, you messed up. I'm going to give you a new covenant, and I'm going to show you My mercy."

In Matthew 19, the Pharisees tested Jesus by asking, in verse 3: "Is it lawful for a man to divorce his wife for any cause?"

And Jesus said, "Don't you know that He who created them both male and female and for this reason shall a man leave his father and mother and cleave to his wife and the two shall become one flesh?"

And then He says, "Therefore, what God has joined together, let no man put asunder."

"Put asunder" in the original Greek indicates to tear apart as the ripping of flesh, flesh as it's hooked on a nail.

Have you ever hooked your flesh on a nail and ripped it? Have you ever seen a news report from war-torn places where there are ravaged arms and ripped flesh? There's no pain like torn flesh.

God uses that analogy to describe the tear of divorce. There are so many members of the Body of Christ who are not walking in the joy of the Lord because of the pain of torn flesh: flesh that is ripped, ligaments that are torn, tendons that are damaged, nerves that are broken, ripped flesh.

BELIEVERS NEED TO STAND UP AND DECLARE THE COVENANT OF MARRIAGE, NOT AN ATTITUDE THAT DECLARES "I'LL BAIL OUT BECAUSE IT ISN'T WORKING OUT." GOD HATES DIVORCE!

Why does God use that analogy for divorce; the tearing apart? Through divorce Satan wants to do damage to society. It's there that he can raise kids in dysfunctional single-parent homes.

I should note here that there are plenty of kids who came from single-family homes that have a wonderful relationship with God. God can do it, but overall the people who come out of single-parent homes don't do well because they have distorted images of God and the Holy Spirit, as well as the family as a unit and themselves. They have a disfigured image of who God is and how the Holy Spirit of God moves.

But you can stop the tearing!

The reason you don't have to have your flesh torn on a nail is because there's one whose flesh was already torn on the nail. Jesus tore His hands, He tore them on a nail. *"He was bruised for our iniquities"* Isaiah 53:5.

As God breaks me with a greater and greater compassion for hurting families and hurting marriages, my prayer is that many might get a greater understanding even of the hurts in their own spouses.

God has dealt with me at times about some of the disappointments that I've placed on Molly, my wife, and that I need to have a greater compassion for her, for the heartache that I cause her. I need to understand with compassion, not just intellectually or logically.

I have to understand that maybe I'm causing some ripping of flesh; maybe I'm causing some piercing. All of us can say that at times we've hurt people close to us.

And so what do we do with that? Do we try to heal those disappointments? Do we try to minister to those points of pain?

You may be away from your spouse right now. You may even be standing for your spouse to come back home. If you learn how to walk in the victorious presence of the glory of God, then God will change your spouse. People can't help but be changed when they step into His presence.

When we establish the glory of God in our lives, each and every one of us is touched. We must avoid the torn flesh of divorce if we intend to live in victory.

America needs people to stand up to declare the covenant relationship of marriage, not an attitude that declares "I'll bail out because it didn't work out."

God hates divorce!

GIFTS FOR THE BRIDE

What does marriage teach us? The longest chapter in the book of Genesis is probably the archetype, the original model from God, as to why He created the institution of marriage. He wanted marriage to be a blessing to us.

"Now Abraham was old, well advanced in age; and the Lord had blessed Abraham in all things. So Abraham said to the oldest servant of his house, who ruled over all that he had, "Please, put your hand under my thigh, and I will make you swear by the Lord, the God of heaven and the God of the earth, that you will not take a wife for my son from the daughters of the Canaanites, among whom I dwell; but you shall go to my country and to my family, and take a wife for my son Isaac."

And the servant said to him, "Perhaps the woman will not be willing to follow me to this land. Must I take your son back to the land from which you came?"

But Abraham said to him, "Beware that you do not take my son back there. The Lord God of heaven, who took me from my father's house and from the land of my family, and who spoke to me and swore to me, saying, 'To your descendants I give this land,' He will send His angel before you, and you shall take a wife for my son from there. And if the woman is not willing to follow you, then you will be released from this oath; only do not take my son back there." Genesis 24:1-8

What happened here? Abraham who is described as the father of all nations chooses his key servant Eliezer to go back and get his son a wife. He chooses to take his oldest servant Eliezer. Eliezer means mighty divine helper. So the father of all nations gets the mighty divine helper to go find a bride for his son. Are you seeing the analogy?

The Holy Spirit is our mighty divine helper. And if Abraham is the father of all nations, than the Holy Spirit is indeed the mighty divine helper.

What is the Holy Spirit's job? It is to call the bride unto the Son and to prepare the bride for the Son.

What does the Holy Spirit do? It says that He does not testify of Himself. Instead He teaches us all things about Jesus, the Son. So here, Eliezer is a type of the Holy Spirit, because he's the most trusted servant whom the father sends to find the bride for his son.

Now what's interesting about this passage, is that the father gives explicit instructions that if the bride is not willing to follow after the son, don't bring the son there.

And sometimes we try to do that in our Christianity. I know I have. You'll say, "What do you mean, try to do what?" Don't you try to take your relationship with Jesus sometimes and mold it or make it fit your form of Christianity? You want Jesus to come with you rather than you follow Jesus.

Each and every one of us is tempted at times to make the cross that Christ has for each and every one of us fit our pattern. We think that God should be a formula or maybe a blessing machine where if we line everything up right, then we should be able to dictate to God what He should do. But the father here explicitly warns the Spirit and says, "No, no, no, don't take the son there."

We get saved, God pulls us out of the pit of darkness and we want to follow but, all of a sudden, we find we want Christ to follow us, adjust to our lifestyle rather than making our life fit Him.

Now what happens here is that Eliezer, the trusted servant, the mighty divine helper is charged with finding a wife for the son. He comes out and is challenged.

Eliezer wanted to know how he would know who the bride is for the son. Eliezer prayed a prayer. He cried out to God for a sign that would show him who the bride is:

"Oh God, my master Abraham has served you faithfully and his desire before he leaves us, is that his son would have the right bride. And I ask that you would give me, his servant, favor Lord, and that as I go into the city, Lord that I would find there a maiden that when 1 ask, "Would you give me to drink?" that she would respond to me "Yes, I will give you to drink and even I will give something to drink to your camels." and I will know Lord that this is the one and that she will agree then to come with me and to leave her family and home and come back to be with my master and his son. I believe you Lord, to help me and I know that you're going to do it."

GOD DID NOT CREATE MARRIAGE TO MAKE YOU HAPPY. GOD CREATED MARRIAGE TO MATURE YOU SPIRITUALLY.

The servant looks for a sign of confirmation upon the bride. The servant wants the Father to confirm the bride for him. And Jesus said if you've seen the Son, you've seen the Father, and so he's charged with finding the right bride for the son.

God indicates in our marriages that the whole reason for marriage is not just to make you happy -- it's so much more.

God did not create marriage to make you happy. God created marriage to mature you spiritually so that you would find a way into His will and that you would understand the relationship that He has for you.

Someone was telling me the other day that God created Eve, and Adam looked at Eve and he said, "Oh, she's so beautiful Lord, why did you make her so beautiful?"

God said to him, "I made her beautiful so that you would love her."

And so Adam reached out and touched Eve, and he said, "Oh, she's so soft, she's so smooth. Why this is wonderful God. Why did you make her so soft and so smooth?"

And God said, "Well, I made her so soft and so smooth so that you would love her Adam."

Then Eve spoke and Adam said, "God, she is stupid. Why did you make her so stupid?"

And God said, "So she would love you, Adam!"

Now that's not scriptural! But God did create the relationship between man and wife because Adam had wonderful relationship in the garden, he had wonderful vertical relationship with God, but God realized that was not enough for him to understand the nature of love that God had for him so he created a horizontal relationship.

God gave him a partner chosen for him in life, a help-mate, so that the two could become one. Through that relationship of love Adam could get a better understanding of God's love for him and also a better understanding about how he is to love. That would increase his life of worship, because we're created in the image of the Creator and it gives Him pleasure when we worship Him.

As we walk in love and as we grow in love in our human lives, do we really increase in love for God?

That's why when the Pharisees asked Jesus, "What is it? What's the greatest commandment?" He said, *"Love the Lord your God with all your heart, with all your soul, with all your strength and with all your mind, and love your neighbor as yourself"* Luke 10:27

We're not equipped to love anyone else, be it our neighbor or our spouse, unless we learn to love ourselves. And we can't really learn to love ourselves until we get a fresh revelation of how much God loves us. So God created relationships.

So, Eliezer journeyed with his master's camels as well as many goods from his master. As he traveled he knew that as he approached the well there might be some people there. Would one of them be the bride for his master's son?

Scripture goes on to tell us that when he approached Nahor he made his camels kneel down outside the city by the well of water at evening time, the time when women go out to draw water.

As was the custom, two ladies approached the well in the evening. Why did these women draw water from the well in the evening. The custom was that women would draw water from the well in the evening after the men and the workers had an opportunity to be at the well. Then they would draw well water so it would be fresh water for dinner at home.

A lady named Rebekah approached the well with her maidservant and they came to draw water. Now it's interesting that Rebekah would be the one that indeed the father had chosen for the son. And so the servant, Eliezer, the mighty divine helper, a type of the Holy Spirit, had prayed that he would find the right bride.

I believe the Holy Spirit is doing that today. I believe that when we become born again, the Holy Spirit groans and intercedes for us according to Romans 8:26. It says that He intercedes for us when we know not what or how we ought to pray, that He intercedes for us with groanings and utterings that we know not of. That's the Holy Spirit groaning to purify the bride.

And he prayed,

"Behold, here I stand by the well of water, and the daughters of the men of the city are coming out to draw water " Genesis 24:13

"And it happened, before he had finished speaking, that behold, Rebekah, who was born to Bethuel, son of Milcah, the wife of Nahor, Abraham's brother, came out with her pitcher on her shoulder. Now the young woman was very beautiful to behold, a virgin; no man had known her. And she went down to the well, filled her pitcher, and came up. And the servant ran to meet her and said, "Please let me drink a little water from your pitcher"

So she said, "Drink, my lord." Then she quickly let her pitcher down to her hand, and gave him a drink. And when she had finished giving him a drink, she said, "I will draw water for your camels also, until they have finished drinking." Then she quickly emptied her pitcher into the trough, ran back to the well to draw water, and drew for all his camels. And the man, wondering at her, remained silent so as to know whether the Lord had made his journey prosperous or not." Genesis 24:15-21

Isn't that the way the Holy Spirit does with us sometimes? We're at that moment of decision. Someone has preached a great message. We maybe don't know the Lord and we wonder, "Is this gospel true? Is this something for us?" And the Holy Spirit remains silent.

Why? Because he doesn't interfere with our will. Yes, God has chosen us, just as He told Moses that the children of Israel were chosen. Just as Ephesians 1:4 and John 15:16 tells us that He chose us.

Sometimes people ask, "When did you find Jesus Christ?" Well, let me tell you, you didn't find Him at all. He chose you.

It's a question of acceptance because God is pleased when we make our free will choice. It's in that quiet time of the Holy Spirit, the servant waiting upon the confirmation of his bride, that it's up to us to make the decision to serve or not.

As he waited, Eliezer realized that the journey was prosperous. And so when the camels had finished drinking, he took a golden nose ring weighing half a shekel and two bracelets for her wrists weighing ten shekels of gold and he offered them to her.

It's interesting to note the symbols that God uses. The servant presents gifts from the father to confirm the bride. Does that happen today? Of course!

I have a tough time with churches where the gifts of the Holy Spirit are not accepted. The gifts of the Holy Spirit are a confirmation of God's blessing on the bride that the Comforter, the Mighty Divine Helper of the Father has indeed said, "Yes, this is a bride befitting, this is a bride willing."

Now, interestingly enough, those gifts alone are not enough. Because what does the Holy Spirit do? The Holy Spirit testifies of Jesus. Even though God may use you in praying for someone and they're healed, don't get all puffed up because it has nothing to do with you.

The reason the servant gives gifts is to confirm the bride so that it might be a testimony of the Son that we are indeed the chosen of the Son.

God gives us gifts so that the world and others may know. And I'm not just talking about the power gifts; there are gifts of faith, gifts of giving, etc.

Those are gifts from the Holy Spirit. Maybe God has given you the gift of giving. You find that sometimes you're giving more of yourself and your finances than you thought possible. That may be a spiritual gift in your life.

Maybe you have great faith when others around you don't see that situation in faith. That's the gift of faith. Maybe at times you feel all of a sudden a supernatural intervention in your being where suddenly you have a wise answer to a situation. That can be God's wisdom given to you to testify to others about His Son and the glory of Jesus.

Will You Go?

And so the servant gives gifts to the bride and then he bowed his head and prayed and worshipped the Lord.

"Blessed be the Lord God of my master Abraham, who has not forsaken His mercy and His truth toward my master. As for me, being on the way, the Lord led me to the house of my master's brethren." Genesis 24:27

So challenging her, he pops the question to her. "Will you follow me to my father's house to be with the son?"

"I will go."

Isn't that the question that the Father asks of us every day? The Holy Spirit tugs at our heart and says, "Will you follow My leading? Will you yield your spirit to the Holy Spirit of God so that you can get to the Father's house for the glory of the Son?"

That's the question we're asked every day and Rebekah's answer is awesome. She simply says, "I will go." And so they journey back to the father's land with gifts preceding them so that from afar people can see that the bride is chosen for the son of the father.

That would be the bride of whom it would be prophesied shortly thereafter that two great nations would come from both Jacob (Israel) and Esau from whom would come many nations.

It's interesting that Rebekah's simple answer is "I will go." You see it's not enough to have accepted Christ. It's not enough to even accept the gifts of God. It's not even enough to be adorned with the gifts of God and operate in them.

The true challenge is the question that the father had asked the servant before he even left, "See if she will be willing to follow."

She says, "I will go."

Does Jesus, in his parting moments, say, "Stay and be my disciples?"

No. What does He say? He says, "Go, and be my disciples."

However, it takes faith, the same type of faith that Abraham had when he stepped out and left his homeland not knowing where he would go to be the father of many nations.

Why? Because God said, "Go."

Are you going and telling the good news in your workplace? Are you going and telling the good news in your family? I have no business preaching the gospel, if the gospel I preach doesn't work in my family. Father Abraham knew that. His most trusted servant is the one he would send to confirm his son's bride and the bride said, "I will go."

> **MARRIAGE IS THE TYPE OF RELATIONSHIP THAT WE AS THE CHURCH ARE TO HAVE WITH THE LORD JESUS CHRIST**

Yet we want God to bless our marriages when we simply are doing what the bride is first supposed to do!

The bottom line is surrender and obedience. Yes, we need to accept the Lord. Yes, we need to press into the Holy Spirit for all that He has for us. But if you don't do anything with it, you become like a monk. You hide yourself and you're no good to anyone. Faith without works is dead.

And then there's no relationship. God has given us marriage for this very reason, so that, like Rebekah, we can say, "Yes," to the will of the Father expressed in our spirit by the Holy Spirit -- to accept His Son as the gift for us. We then receive the gifts from the Father so that we might be able to minister back unto Jesus Christ.

That's what God wants us to do. God has not given us marriage simply to make us happy, not simply to procreate or create children. Marriage is the type of relationship that we as the church are to have with the Lord Jesus Christ.

Jesus said, "Blessed are you for you have not seen and yet believe."

Has anyone alive today ever seen Jesus in the flesh? No. We have not seen Him yet we believe, so we are blessed!

Rebekah had not seen Isaac, but yet her spirit bore witness because she was willing. Willing to serve even before she knew her place of service, and that was the confirmation that she indeed was the bride. The willingness that not only would she offer him a drink, but that she had the servant's heart and was willing to serve and water his camels for him. That was the confirmation in the Holy Spirit that there was a willingness to serve.

And if we can develop strong and mighty couples for God's glory, where each husband and wife is willing to serve each other, then other people will see that service and the confirming power of God manifested. The gifts of the Holy Spirit will be made evident in those couples to where others will say, "Yes! That's the bride of Christ!"

That's the body of Christ. It's not a hypocritical religious tradition or a system of man. These are people who are living out what God has called them to. These are people who have been called.

Now here's the key. Rebekah said, "I will go." She stood in the presence of the Holy Spirit and the Holy Spirit pulled at her heart and asked her a question.

And her response was "I will go."

Will you go? Will you do what it takes to make your marriage testify of the goodness of God? Will you submit your spirit to the Holy Spirit of God so that others would see His confirming gifting, operating in your life and marriage?

Will you go?

Is God in Your Marriage?

PART TWO
OUR POSITION IN MARRIAGE

WHO IS YOUR HUSBAND?

Are you ready for a deep and scriptural truth concerning communicating as a married couple? It has to do with communicating your love one for another but many people have never learned to express their love at all.

Isaiah 54:5 says, *"For your Maker is your husband."* That's amazing.

Right there, God says we are all in a feminine relationship to Him. That's difficult for a lot of men to deal with.

God is our husband.

It's also difficult for some women to deal with because when they hear the word "husband" it reminds them of wounds, pain and unfulfilled expectations.

The images we have might be really contrary to what God is saying here when He says, *"For your Maker is your husband, The Lord of hosts is His name; And your Redeemer is the Holy One of Israel;*

He is called the God of the whole earth. For the Lord has called you Like a woman forsaken and grieved in spirit, Like a youthful wife when you were refused," Says your God.

"For a mere moment I have forsaken you, But with great mercies I will gather you. With a little wrath I hid My face from you for a moment; But with everlasting kindness I will have mercy on you," Says the Lord, your Redeemer." Isaiah 54:5-8

The challenge of viewing God as our husband is that we have such an imperfect view of husbands. As men we have an imperfect view of ourselves as husbands. And women have an imperfect view of men as husbands.

If we look at God's role in our lives as husband we will really find out what it means to view God as our husband. We'll understand what the scripture is all about.

It's difficult for us as men to think that someone would be our husband. A man's psychology thinks that part of a husband's role is to fulfill his wife physically. So it's almost perverse to think of God as a husband, as someone who would want to meet our needs physically.

God does want to meet our needs physically as men. Not in a sexual connotation. But He wants to meet all of our needs. Once we really see God as our husband then it's a revealing truth in our lives.

Why do women get married? Because they have that deep down desire for intimacy, for unity, for harmony, to be loved and to be desired. Really, that's what all of us want. We all want that intimacy, unity and harmony. We don't want to feel alone. We want to feel together and one. We want to feel complete, to desire and to be desired.

In fact, when you were first attracted to your spouse, one of the things that made them open up to your attraction to them was the fact that they felt that you desired them.

What God is saying in this passage is "Your Maker is your husband." It's interesting that He chooses the word, "Maker".

He defines Himself in the realm of our creation. He says the Creator of the universe is the one who is desirous of you. That's a powerful truth. So many today relish this false humility of "Oh, we're so unworthy of God's love."

But He says the Creator of the universe is desirous of you! Your Maker wants that intimacy, that unity, harmony, close relationship, that feeling of being loved and of loving you. And that's why God wants to be your husband.

If we look around our society we see everyone has that same basic desire for intimacy and desire. Just flip through the radio stations and you'll hear most of the groups today sing about love. Country music is often about broken love. It's sad. Popular music culture cries out the heart of man that desires love, unity and harmony.

Everybody is looking for love. We all want it. But romantic love is really irrational. When we're attracted to someone and desirous of them, it's irrational.

Different types of love are rational. For example, parental love is rational. When you have children your love for them is rational; flesh of my flesh, blood of my blood, I have a natural responsibility; it's something that exhibits part of my characteristics that I look for. There's a natural aspect to parental love.

But courting love really is irrational. It doesn't make sense. Wooing doesn't make sense sometimes. Sometimes we do goofy little things that if we did them in the presence of anyone else, we'd be totally embarrassed. Just think of how we refer to our spouse sometimes. I call Molly, "honeybunch" and "snug" and other names like that. Honeybunch means nothing. What is a honeybunch? I've never seen a bunch of honey. It's totally irrational. It doesn't mean anything.

IF WE LOOK AROUND OUR SOCIETY WE SEE EVERYONE HAS THAT SAME BASIC DESIRE FOR INTIMACY AND DESIRE

I have a phoneline that comes into my office on which Molly is usually the only one to call. Someone else got a hold of that number and I picked up the line and said, "Hi honeybunch!" And it wasn't honeybunch. I was embarrassed.

Everyone has terms of endearment that you relate to your spouse that could be embarrassing. They seem irrational in the world. But that's what wooing love is. It's irrational.

The majesty of God saying, "For your Maker is your husband", is that His love for you is both irrational (wooing) and rational (parental). In no other relationship can we have both types of love fulfilled.

That's why God's example of love as a husband is a high call, a high example for husbands. Our love toward our spouse is to be both irrational (wooing) and rational (parental, covering, secure and nurturing).

And likewise wives, if you understand that God's love for you, as your husband, is both irrational and rational, then part of your love toward your husband is rational and irrational.

When you first came to know the Lord Jesus Christ was everything about it rational? Probably not. There are a lot of paradoxes in God's kingdom. A lot of things seem to make no sense. It's irrational,

But yet it was rational when you came to accept Jesus Christ, that He died for your sins and that the Maker of the universe had an unfailing, unconditional love for you. That was rational.

But a lot of other things in the Word of God seem to be irrational. Love your enemies. That doesn't seem rational. Give and you shall receive. It doesn't seem rational.

We must realize that God's love for us is both rational and irrational. And so it is with our love for our spouse.

I like the old Hebrew proverb that says, "Don't fall in love, rise in love." Think about that. I don't want to go backward or downward. I want my love for my wife to raise me up to a higher level.

That's what God is saying when He says, "Your Maker is your husband." He wants you to recognize that the love He has for you is higher than the love of any single person.

When we have courting love, it's intoxicating. We're intoxicated by love when we're desirous to another. In other words, when we realize someone else desires us there's an intoxicating effect. That's why sometimes people fall into affairs. Maybe they're no longer experiencing that intoxication, not feeling that expression of desire from their spouse and suddenly someone else is expressing desire toward them.

It's almost intoxicating that we should be loved by someone, that someone should have such a desire for us. Courting love is something that awakens within you. It's not there all the time. It awakens during adolescence. By adolescence I mean a time of maturing, not puberty.

That's not when courting love awakens within you, that's physical love.

But courting love awakens within you at the time when as a little boy, you stop throwing rocks at the little girls and start to get embarrassed around them.

Courting love gets embarrassed around the opposite sex because you know God has someone for you. You know God has chosen someone of the opposite sex.

You might not know it consciously, but innately, when you waken as an adolescent, you start to realize God has chosen someone of the opposite sex.

You may not even know it's God, but you know there's someone out there that will be your mate and you'll be desirously attracted to them. And your desire is to be desired by that person. That too is intoxicating.

No Human Model

The ultimate marriage, however, is not dependant upon any human model. The ultimate human marriage is dependant upon our yearning, on our irrational desire for love.

Jesus is already looking at us that way.

If we could only realize that Jesus looks at us and says, "Wow, I desire you. I desire you greatly! Irrationally." Why would we be desirous to Jesus? Why should we be desirous to Jesus? Yet He looks at us with great and intense desire. He says I want to attract you to Me.

You know what amazes me is people asking, "When did you find Jesus Christ?" To me that's weird. It sounds like something you found in a dumpster outside a restaurant. When did you find Jesus Christ? Or did you find Him? I'm not sure I ever found Him. I think He found me.

He was attracting me all the time. He was desirous after me. By the Holy Spirit of God, He was wooing me and courting me all my life. That's what God does.

Even when a person is far away from the Lord, the Holy Spirit is still attempting to court him, and woo him and let him know He is desirous of him. The Holy Spirit has a desire to draw you to Him.

The Holy Spirit wants you to meet your Maker. And when you meet your Maker, the next step is to find out your Maker is your husband.

When you find out your Maker is your husband, you have this understanding of how awesome God's love is for you because none of us deserve God's love. But yet we do. By the Bible's standards we do, but in our own standards we think we don't deserve God's love.

He says He has not abandoned us. In Isaiah 54:7 He says, *"For a mere moment I have forsaken you, But with great mercies I will gather you."*

Majesty and Mercy

What is it that's amazing about God as our husband? If our Maker is our husband, He represents, as God, both majesty and mercy. Men, if you can understand that as a husband, you are to represent to your wife both majesty and mercy, this could transform your marriage.

Your wife will receive your majesty, authority, rulership, leadership, if she receives your mercy. None of us received Jesus as King of Kings and Lord of Lords unless we first accepted His mercy and forgiveness for our sins. That's the way it is in our homes, too.

As husbands we have to reflect mercy toward our spouse. We have to be constantly responding in mercy.

Throughout God's Word there are examples of merciful love -- the anointing of love -- that breaks the yoke of bondage. The bondage Satan tries to put on each and every one of us is the belief that we are not loved.

Yet God says, "Your Maker is your husband." He's creating covenant with you.

Why would God want that everlasting covenant with you? Because He loves you and He created you. You are fearfully and wonderfully made, created in His image. He deemed that from the beginning of time.

When man messed it up, He redeemed it. Even from creation, He knew He would have a plan of redemption, He would buy us back by Jesus' love. Why? Because we got away from His love. But His covenant didn't change. His love toward us didn't change. God's love has never failed. It's there all the time. His covenant is everlasting.

When He says He is your Maker and husband, that means He is not committing adultery. That's why He said, *"Thou shall not commit adultery."* Man commits adultery, but God cannot in His perfect form commit adultery. He cannot betray you. His love for you is pure.

Why does God say not to commit adultery? Not so much because of the personal pain it causes us but it's sin in our life that separates us from Him. We break our covenant with God. He has not broken His covenant. His love is still there for us and His love is everlasting.

This is a powerful truth if you can recognize God's love, as a husband for you, then it will release you. Perhaps you don't understand and haven't received God's love. As a result you don't know how to love your spouse.

"You shall love the Lord your God with all your heart, with all your soul, with all your strength, and with all your mind, and your neighbor as yourself" Luke 10:27

You can't love yourself unless you recognize God's love as your spouse. Since He determined His love at creation, made a covenant and had a plan for redemption, then He says, *"The Lord of hosts is His name; and your Redeemer is the Holy One of Israel."* Isaiah 54:5

Now we understand who the Redeemer is. Your Redeemer is the Holy One of Israel. Jesus came to redeem us, buy back the love of God so that we would be out of wrong standing and back in good standing with Him.

"He is called the God of the whole earth. For the Lord has called you like a woman forsaken and grieved in spirit, like a youthful wife when you were refused," says your God." Isaiah 54:5-6

God is healing relationships. In the relationships He is healing, He is calling people back. He's saying, have you felt like a person who's been rejected? Throughout our lives we're taught rejection. Society teaches us rejection and the satanic deception is that we have self-rejection.

Rejection occurs because our flesh gets in the way. Our flesh perverts our God given appetite.

God has given us an appetite for sex. When we pervert that, it's perversion.

God has given us an appetite to eat. When it's perverted it becomes gluttony. God made millions and millions of taste buds. Why? Because in His creation He was expressing extravagance. God didn't have to create us with taste buds. He could have created us with a tongue that just consumed what was needed for survival. But instead, He wants us to enjoy.

His creation expresses His extravagant love for us. Think of the toucan with a large colorful beak and the parrots that come in so many different colors. That has nothing to do with defense or survival. It's God's extravagant expression of love and beauty toward us and His world.

God wants to express His extravagance toward us. And in the same way that those are symbols of His extravagant love for the whole earth, He expresses His extravagant love for us through personality.

All of creation expresses personality. There's personality in the bird kingdom and personality in your taste buds. Our daughter, Emily, likes all kinds of food. She liked Italian, Thai, Indian and Mexican -- all kinds of spicy foods that she started liking at the age of 3 1/2. She liked hot salsa with chips. God's given her those taste buds. Maybe they're an acquired taste, but nonetheless she has those taste buds. She has personality.

You have foods you like and dislike. God has given you those appetites. If you pervert them they become gluttony and it becomes sin. So God has given all of us appetites that are a reflection of His love and the beauty in creation for us. But when we get them out of line with Him, they become sin and separate us from Him.

GOD THINKS WE ARE SO BEAUTIFUL. HE IS ATTRACTED TO US.

God thinks we're so beautiful. He's attracted to us. Think about that. He's desirous of us. That's so wonderful.

It's like parenting. Parenting occurs when a couple falls in love (or rises in love), gets married and now their expression of love bursts forth and there's a physical union. All of a sudden, the woman swells up until she's about to burst and out comes an expression of their love.

And what happens? You find you have a greater capacity to love. The pressure of love is such that it must love all the more and more and more and more.

All of creation expresses His extravagance for us and expresses His love for us.

When we understand His love is there for us, then we can understand why that love is there. If you looked at parenting totally in the natural, it might not be so attractive.

If you were to tell a woman, "Here, sign this contract. I'll help you swell up to more than one and one half of your size, help an incredible event occur where you'll practically be ripped open and then out will come this little monster who will become an emperor. You'll become his slave, waking up in the middle of the night, immediately having to take care of his every need or he'll scream at you."

How many ladies would sign that kind of contract? The reason they do sign the contract is because of the extravagance of love. They understand the extravagance of God's love and their ability to pour out love into that child.

Women who have a child all of a sudden glow. They have a new expression of who they are. They understand their being because now the pressure of wanting love is exploded in them. And the pressure to pour out their love is now expressed through them.

Expressions of Unconditional Love

When you have a baby and they first smile at you or first audibly laugh, that's a melting experience. It's an expression of unconditional love. That child just expressed his love toward you and it melts your heart. It has nothing to do with that contract to parent.

So often we look at God's love through our natural senses and not through our spiritual senses. When the parent looks at that child, he has great grace toward that child. We all have grace toward our children. We all have the ability to forgive. We all pour out our love over and over again. But our society so hardens our courting love that people become lax in their forgiveness toward their spouse.

Maybe it's because we have higher demands on maturity. But God doesn't have those higher demands on our maturity as a precondition of His grace. He says, "I will never leave you nor forsake you, -- no matter what you've done as a spouse. I will not commit adultery. You may commit adultery, but I will not."

That's why the Hosea and Gomer relationship is a type of God's love. That's why "for your Maker is your husband" expresses that He draws up that covenant.

So God's original plan, when He expressed covenant love for us is that He will not commit adultery. He will never leave us. Once you have accepted Christ, you, as a type of the bride of Christ, have made God your husband. Then you have to recognize that His love is always there for you, regardless of what you've done.

Our courting communication in life is just a shadow of God's love for us. If we can dwell and focus on God's love for us as our husband, then we'll have more love to pour out to our spouse. We'll have more love that we'll be able to deal with, husband and wife.

In Song of Solomon 1:5 there is an expression of God's love. The Shulamite woman in this passage is a type of the bride of Christ. Verse 5 says, *"I am dark, but lovely, 0 daughters of Jerusalem, like the tents of Kedar, like the curtains of Solomon. Do not look upon me, because I am dark, because the sun has tanned me."*

She is saying here don't look upon me because I am sunburned. That's the way we feel sometimes toward God.

We don't accept God's love because we feel inadequate. We may be tanned; we're looking good. But then when we're naked the red lines from our burn don't look so good. Maybe we're sunburned or uncomfortable because we don't look just right. We're not perfect.

"My mother's sons were angry with me; they made me the keeper of the vineyards, but my own vineyard I have not kept." Song of Solomon 1:6 This is an expression of our feeling unfaithful.

Who Is Your Husband?

Sometimes we don't receive God's love because we feel like we've been unfaithful in keeping that which has been entrusted to us.

Almost each and every one of us, if we examine what has been entrusted us throughout our whole lives, there have been times of unfaithfulness. But the beloved lets the Shulamite woman know that doesn't matter. He loves her nonetheless. It doesn't matter.

Has your spouse ever been unfaithful to you? Each one has been unfaithful to our spouse at one time or another. And I don't mean adultery, necessarily. It might be unfaithfulness in our unwavering love. Perhaps in a moment of anger or as we snap at our spouse or begin a totally stupid spat - that's an example of our unfaithfulness. We haven't tended our vineyard that's been entrusted to us.

He's Trying to Bless You

Is it because we feel we're unworthy of our spouse's love? I don't think so. Often it's because we're demanding of our spouse's love. But when it comes to our relationship with God, sometimes we feel so unworthy of His love.

Human love has messed up our concept of God's love for ourselves. Whatever circumstance you're in, don't let your insecurity in God's love stop you. Because whatever circumstance you're in, God looks at you now and He's trying to bless you in that circumstance.

Even if you are separated from your spouse, or going through a financial nightmare, God is looking at you in that situation and saying, "OK. Press in. I want to bless you." That's His whole desire. He's an unconditionally loving husband. He wants to bless you no matter what your circumstance is right now

It may be circumstances you've thrown yourself into because you reap what you sow due to sin in your life. But He wants you to recognize that once you have sinned, you need to repent and change so He can bless you again. God has forgiven us, however, sometimes we don't forgive ourselves of our sin.

Have you ever looked at yourself? What image do you have of yourself? The only way I can see myself is if I cross my eyes. I can see my nose because it's big enough. That's the only way I can look at myself.

Most other times we look at ourselves through a mirror and it's only a reflection of ourselves. Our human relationships are reflections of ourselves. Yet God wants to reflect to us how He views us.

How does He do that?

Through the eyes of Jesus. And the eyes of Jesus are pure. When we look into Jesus' eyes we see pure love. We don't see the reflection we see in all of our other relationships. We're comfortable singing about our love toward God.

Many praise and worship choruses in churches today are about our love toward God, but we sing very little about His love toward us - other than the all time hit 'Jesus Loves Me'. We teach that to little kids.

WE OFTEN DON'T ACCEPT LOVE BECAUSE WE MEASURE OURSELVES AGAINST IDEALS

Why? Because little children learn that openly because they haven't faced all that self-rejection. They receive it and sing, "Jesus loves me this I know" with a pure heart because they understand God's love and they sing it out.

But because the way the world treats you and reflects toward you all this self-rejection, you think you're ugly and unlovable. God doesn't view you as ugly. He's attracted to you, no matter what the world does to you.

We often don't accept love because we measure ourselves against ideals. Every generation has it's own ideals. The word ideal comes from the word for idol. So we create an ideal based on an idol. When we're 12, 13, 14 or whatever-years old, that which is popular that day becomes an ideal: the way one dresses, the way one looks. Those become ideals. It's really idolatry.

Then we measure ourselves against that standard and we don't measure up. We begin to reject ourselves and we don't live up to God's love for us. We don't accept God's love for us because we're not accepting our own love for ourselves. We've rejected our own ability to receive love.

We have a lot of scar tissue and a lot of wounds of rejection that limit our ability to receive from God. But what God wants to do is to take all that away and let you know that He is your Maker and your husband. His love toward you is pure. You are desirous to Him in every aspect.

He wants to look into our face. Song of Solomon 2:14 says, "O my dove, in the clefts of the rock, in the secret places of the cliff let me see your face, let me hear your voice; for your voice is sweet, and your face is lovely." This is an expression of God's love for us.

Jesus is looking at us like a dove. A dove is a symbol of purity, peace and harmlessness. That's how Jesus looks at us.

Yet where does He see us? He sees us in the clefts of the rock. Hardly a romantic image. Some little crack in the rock where that dove has hidden itself for warmth, safety and protection -- that's the way God sees us.

He's saying, "Oh my dove, my precious little harmless thing, my beautiful person. You're hiding out in the clefts of the rock. Don't hide from Me in the secret place of the cliff. Let Me see your countenance. Let Me see your face."

So many of us don't want God or anyone else to see our face. That's why so many women cover up with so much makeup. They don't want anyone to see their face. A lot of women won't leave home without their makeup on. Perhaps they haven't understood the redeemed love of God in their life.

Why? Because, He says, "Come out of that crag, come out of that hiding place, let Me see your face." What He's saying is, "Your face is so beautiful to Me, it's desirous to Me. Let Me see your face. I don't care what anybody else says. You are fearfully and wonderfully made. You're unique."

Today, God knows you and loves you just the way you are. He says, "Let Me see your face, you're beautiful." That's God's love for us. He wants us to recognize how much He loves us. Often we sing about our love for God, but we sing very little of His love for us and that's worship unto Him. As He said, *"Let me hear your voice; for your voice is sweet, and your face is lovely."*

What happened in the garden? Adam and Eve fell and what is the first thing God says?

"Where are you?"

He wanted to see their faces, but Adam and Eve had hidden their faces in shame. In their own spirit they knew they did wrong and it caused them to hide their faces in shame.

Some people live that way, day in and day out. They live with their own sense of self-rejection because they've never recognized God as their husband. They've never recognized His unconditional love for them. There should be no shame.

The same holds true for you. He finds your face lovely, appealing and wonderful. He understands your broken and harmless condition as you hide in the cleft of the rock. He wants to love you. When you open up to His love, you receive His love. Then you get that pressure of love inside you that you can pour out to your spouse.

We have terms of endearment for each other where we whisper sweet nothings. What does that mean? That's irrational love -- the same type of irrational love that God has for us. It draws Him to us and makes us desirous for Him.

As we whisper sweet nothings in our spouse's ear it makes them feel desired and loved. That's what God is doing. He's whispering sweet nothings in your ear. He wants you to be vulnerable and sense the heart of God.

Isaiah 62:2 says, *"The Gentiles shall see your rightteousness, and all kings your glory. You shall be called by a new name, which the mouth of the Lord will name."*

God came up with the term "anointed one", Christ, and we're called Christians. God's chosen people are not just the Jews. God's chosen people are Christians. He's called us by a new name to express His love for us.

"You shall also be a crown of glory in the hand of the Lord, and a royal diadem in the hand of your God.

You shall no longer be termed Forsaken, nor shall your land any more be termed Desolate; but you shall be called Hephzibah, and your land Beulah."

Isaiah 62:3-4

Hephzibah means my delight is in her, and Beulah means married. You shall be called my delight is in her and married.

"For the Lord delights in you, and your land shall be married. For as a young man marries a virgin, so shall your sons marry you; and as the bridegroom rejoices over the bride, so shall your God rejoice over you."
Isaiah 62:4-5

God Rejoices Over You

God is rejoicing over you. Maybe you're trapped in some sin that you fall into again and again and again and you're hidden. So in shame, you're not letting the love of God wash you. Maybe that's why you don't have the discipline to be in His Word or to praise Him and talk to Him in prayer. Maybe you struggle with that because you don't recognize His love.

Maybe you don't recognize that He's saying "I want to see your face. No matter that you've sinned."

In the same way He called out to Adam, "Where are you?" He's saying, "Let me see your countenance from the cleft of the rock."

Marriage is a unique relationship. It's not conformity. Each one of us has a unique relationship with God. We don't have to all be the same because we're Christians, so it is with our spouse, too. Each marriage is an individual and unique relationship. It's one that God has because God loves each of you individually.

God's love for you is totally unique in that way. God wants to bless you. He wants to trust you so that you might inherit even more. How much does He have for us that He would have us inherit? First however, He wants us to pour out our love.

When we speak of that wonderful desirous love our language is inadequate. That's why the world attempts to reflect love in art, music, poetry and words that seem distant. But there are no words that can truly express God's love for us because we're fearfully and wonderfully made. And He chose to say that "your Maker is your husband."

If you can grasp this truth then God will release you and allow His love in your heart in such a way that you won't be as demanding of your spouse's love. When you receive God's love you'll have more love to pour out into your spouse. Just allow God's love to wash over you. Just make it a moment between you and God. Allow your worship to go up to God.

If you focus on God's love for you and let God minister His love to you, the love of your spouse won't matter that much. In other words, you won't depend on their love to the degree where it controls you. And you'll have more love to pour into your spouse.

If both you and your spouse allow God's love to wash you to where you pour out His love into each other's life, then all the past hurt, rejection and even self-rejection can be healed.

Maybe you've held yourself up to that high standard and said, "I'm not beautiful." God says you're beautiful and adorable. He's totally desirous of you. God wants you just as you are: fearfully and wonderfully made. He wants to minister to each and every one of your needs, no matter what your circumstance is.

He wants to bless you and trust you with more and more so He can continue to bless you and increase His inheritance for you. As He pours out His love for you, you'll receive a greater love. Take some time to receive God's love for you, and get ready to become a conduit of His love to others, especially to your spouse.

THE DEVOTION OF A YOUTHFUL BRIDE

Jeremiah is a young prophet. He's just been called out by God and he says, "Who, who me God? I'm but a youth." Its the eleventh year of the reign of King Josiah. King Josiah became king over the land at the ripe old age of 16. As he matured quickly in those eleven years, he led what was one of the greatest revivals of young people in all of history.

He brought young people back to a desire and a hunger for God out of a realm of idolatry. But he did it with the help of Jeremiah. And so, in the second chapter of Jeremiah, God has just called Jeremiah to preach his first sermon. He feels unworthy and challenged, because his first sermon is to be a rebuke of the people of the land.

Jeremiah 2:1-19 (NIV):

The word of the LORD came to me:

"Go and proclaim in the hearing of Jerusalem: 'I remember the devotion

71

of your youth, how as a bride you loved me and followed me through the desert, through a land not sown.

Israel was holy to the Lord, the firstfruits of his harvest; all who devoured her were held guilty, and disaster overtook them," declares the Lord.

Hear the word of the Lord, 0 house of Jacob, all you clans of the house of Israel.

This is what the Lord says: "What fault did your fathers find in me, that they strayed so far from me? They followed worthless idols and became worthless themselves.

They did not ask, 'Where is the Lord, who brought us up out of Egypt and led us through the barren wilderness, through a land of deserts and rifts, a land of drought and darkness, a land where no one travels and no one lives?'

I brought you into a fertile land to eat its fruit and rich produce. But you came and defiled my land and made my inheritance detestable.

The priests did not ask, 'Where is the Lord?' Those who deal with the law did not know me; the leaders rebelled against me. The prophets prophesied by Baal, following worthless idols.

"Therefore I bring charges against you again," declares the Lord. "And I will bring charges against your children's children.

Cross over to the coasts of Kittim and look, send to Kedar and observe closely; see if there has ever been anything like this:

Has a nation ever changed its gods? (Yet they are not gods at all.) But my people have exchanged their Glory for worthless idols.

"Be appalled at this, Oh heavens, and shudder with great horror," declares the Lord.

'My people have committed two sins: They have forsaken me, the spring of living water, and have dug their own cisterns, broken cisterns that cannot hold water'.

Is Israel a servant, a slave by birth? Why then has he become plunder?

Lions have roared; they have growled at him. They have laid waste his land; his towns are burned and deserted.

Also, the men of Memphis and Tahpanhes have shaved the crown of your head.

Have you not brought this on yourselves by forsaking the Lord your God when he led you in the way?

Now why go to Egypt to drink water from the Shihor? And why go to Assyria to drink water from the River?

Your wickedness will punish you; your backsliding will rebuke you. Consider then and realize how evil and bitter it is for you when you forsake the Lord your God and have no awe of me," declares the Lord, the Lord Almighty.

Then in Jeremiah 2:32-37 (NIV):

"Does a maiden forget her jewelry, a bride her wedding ornaments? Yet my people have forgotten me, days without number.

How skilled you are at pursuing love! Even the worst of women can learn from your ways. On your clothes men find the lifeblood of the innocent poor, though you did not catch them breaking in.

Yet in spite of all this you say, "I am innocent, he is not angry with me."

But I will pass judgment on you because you say, "I have not sinned."

Why do you go about so much, changing your ways? You will be disappointed by Egypt as you were by Assyria. You will also leave that place with your hands on your head, for the Lord has rejected those you trust, you will not be helped by them.

In this, the very first message that Jeremiah preaches, he begins by lambasting the people for forgetting the devotion of their youth.

Let's draw the analogy today and make it personal to ourselves, that is, to the devotion of our youthful spiritual lives once we were born again.

When you first got saved, you had that awesome zeal. There's new life, there's that energy in you, but then, people of the religious system begin to sap you of that lifeblood and that strength. So often people step into the river. But God says here through Jeremiah, "Why do you want to drink from the river in Egypt? I'm the living water. Two things I have against you, you've forsaken Me, the spring of living water."

Jesus says, "From your innermost being shall flow living water" and that's what we forsake. We forget our first love, the very same thing occurred in the church at Ephesus, they forgot their first love of leading people to Jesus Christ. They forgot their first love of sharing what God had done with them.

He makes an analogy and says that as a bride. "You loved me and followed me through the desert."

When you first became born again, your devotion was to Him and yet you were in a desert place. You were in a wilderness that you didn't know.

You came out of the world and now you're thrown into the Christian culture. If you were like me, I didn't understand being washed by the blood right away. When they sang that, I thought, "Man, this is weird."

Then the church people used words like "sanctification" and "fellowship" and "edification" and "admonish" and "exhort."

I thought I had had a good vocabulary before that time, but I didn't understand what they were talking about. I was in a wilderness; I was in a desert place.

I was a youth that God had called out and in my innermost being was that living water. I was devoted to Him.

"Wow, this is truth. I've found what I've always been looking for."

Getting Used to It

But then, like a bride, one begins to become accustomed to the place where you are and the desert becomes home.

Pretty soon you become accustomed to the radical change and the cold nights and you become accustomed to gusts of wind and sand in your eyes. You accept the discomfort of the desert rather than maintaining the devotion of your youth to be in that river of living water.

What had happened to the children of Israel is what happens to a lot of us in our Christian lives. We step out into that river -- into the living water -- but we stay so close to the banks that we spend all of our time fighting off the debris.

In a river the debris is near the banks, such as driftwood, also there's mud where your feet get stuck. But if you step out deeper into the full flow of God, the Holy Spirit comes in and all of a sudden there's no garbage to deal with. It's just you and the flow of the river.

In 1982, I had the privilege of going white-water rafting on the Ocoee River outside of Chattanooga, Tennessee. It had been a big snow year, so the river was raging.

I was a travel journalist at the time and I was assigned to cover this white-water 12-man raft with a guide in the back. But I didn't have the guts to tell my editor that I did not know how to swim.

This is the second fastest river in the United States. You have to wear a helmet, life vest and all kind of equipment. You must go through a three-hour class the morning before you go out on the river. They have a state police officer in the room during the class to make sure that you've received the training and that you have sat through the whole three-hour class.

The instructor shows you videotapes and tells you things to do if you should get thrown from the boat: immediately tuck in your knees and put your head down with your helmet between your knees, The force of the river will throw you out to the sides. If you stay loose and don't get in a tuck when you are thrown, you're going to get an arm ripped off by a rock or a branch or something like that. So they are intimidating you during this three-hour training.

And here I am, not knowing how to swim.

At the end of the training, the instructor said, "Okay, I just want to get an idea of what kind of level of swimmers we have here. How many of you are lifeguards?"

There were about 36 people in the room, I think there were three rafts going that day and two guys raised their hands; they were lifeguards.

The instructor then asked, "How many of you consider yourselves expert swimmers?" More hands went up.

"How many of you intermediate? How many of you beginner?" At the end, he looked at me and said, "You sir, you didn't raise your hand. How well do you swim?"

And I said, "I don't,"

Every head in the room turned and looked at me and thought, "What's with this guy?"

We then began the ride of our life. We got in and they strapped our feet in the raft.

Unless you obey the instructions of the guide you imperil everybody else in the boat. Now you must know the other eleven people in the boat were not thrilled that I was in their boat!

Sometimes it's that way in our Christian life. There's a newborn Christian and he doesn't know how to swim. We're afraid to minister to him and to love him because he might not understand the culture.

Yet, we were like him. Because others didn't minister to us when we were newborns, we didn't immediately move from milk to meat and get into the deeper things of the Lord.

God doesn't thrust us out into the middle of the river where His flow and His Holy Spirit takes us and leads us. Instead, we're left standing in the mucky mire fighting off the debris of religious people, self-righteous people and people who don't have an understanding of the nature and character of God. They've been stuck in the mud all their lives rather than the flow of the Holy Spirit.

We have to make a decision, like a youthful bride, to follow wherever our Lord leads us -- to take the risky plunge and obey before we find ourselves in the full flow of the river of life.

IN CHRISTIAN LIFE OR IN MARRIAGE, BEING A TEAM PLAYER MEANS BEING A SERVANT; IT'S THE PATH TO FULFILLMENT.

Jeremiah is talking to this kind of people. Get back to the devotion of your youth. Get back to that exciting energy you had.

When we went down that river in Tennessee, about halfway down the river (and it was a three-hour ride that to me seemed like about eleven minutes), the guide yelled "hard left" and everybody would lean out the left side of the boat and row hard. He would yell, "hard right", "smooth left", "smooth right", and with all these instructions, you had to go along.

There was a fear of not participating in the community that would imperil you. Since there was a fear that you might miss or react too slowly to the voice of the guide, everyone obeyed.

How would the bride of Christ be if we lived in that kind of holy fear?

Jeremiah lambasts the people for all their disobedience, and then he says for the Lord, speaking prophetically, "You've lost my fear."

Why did they lose the fear?

He says several things occurred.

"Is Israel my servant?" They had lost the attitude of a servant. You can't fulfill what God has for you in the body of Christ or in your marriage unless you become a team player. This means being a servant.

It's the very nature of the Lord Jesus Christ! At the Last Supper, one of the most profound moments in all of history, Jesus is sitting there sharing with his disciples, instituting communion. Jesus says, *"Do this in remem¬brance of Me."*

So here He is at the Last Supper, ready to institute this great ritual and in Luke 22:24, it says: *"Now there was also a dispute among them, as to which of them should be considered the greatest."*

Ambition Often Intrudes on Humility

Often that occurs in the body of Christ and within our marriage as a microcosm of the body of Christ. At significant moments in your life, when the presence of God shows up there is often an interruption of rivalry. When Jesus was instituting communion at the Last Supper, do you think the presence of God was there? Of course.

So, rivalry rose among them as to which of them was the greatest. The enemy will do that in your marriage. He will at different times try to make you gain control, try to make you think that it's time for you to possess territory. When the presence of God shows up, that's when humility should be there.

The disciples gathered for this great moment in history and when humility should have abounded, ambition intruded. That's the way the enemy

77

always works. When God moves mightily in our life, sometimes we want to sing and shout and dance about. That's fine. There are times for celebration. But there are also times for you to come into that sovereign presence of God and feel the presence of the Holy Spirit. It's a humble moment. Humility should abound but often ambition intrudes.

In the upper room Jesus answers his disciples and says, "Yes, you have many benefactors yet I am among you as one who serves."

Servanthood. That's why Jeremiah in rebuking them says, "You don't have the devotion of your youth. You're not like that newfound bride that loves Me. You're not like that anymore."

Lack of servanthood will pull you away from the presence of God.

Stop Listening to Lions

The second thing Jeremiah says is that young lions have roared and you have listened to them.

We all listen to different voices. The voice might be an impression on your spirit. There's a battle for our souls between light and darkness and those voices are talking to us.

God wants to impress upon your spirit what He would say. But we listen to young lions. *"Your enemy the devil prowls around like a roaring lion looking for someone to devour"* I Peter 5:8 NIV

We must realize that a roaring male lion is a lazy liar. If you study the way lions live, you'll find the king of the jungle to be deceptive. He's got a big mane and looks mean and tough but he doesn't do the hunting. He lies around and has sex while all the women do the hunting. To relate as men to lions is a perversion of God's plan.

The lion of Judah, Jesus, is the servant leader who serves the weaker vessel. That's the original plan.

When a young lion roars, he's learning his vocal strength. By the time he becomes a full-grown male lion, his vocal strength is awesome. If you stand in front of a full-grown male lion when he roars, the force of his roar is greater than those sub-woofer bass cabinets used at concerts. The force of a male lion's roar can actually knock you down. A full-grown male lion roaring can be heard up to five miles away in the Serengeti plains of Kenya. Yet, it's mostly a threat. It's only a lie, a lazy deception, used in the hope that others will be frightened into doing something stupid.

Like America today, the people of Judah (the tribe of praise that Jeremiah's addressing) have listened to the young lions. They've listened to those little demonic voices that say, "Don't be so committed to God. Come here, there's some sinful pleasure over here. And you know what? Don't just pray and seek God. I think you'd better manipulate your spouse a little bit to make that happen rather than trust God."

Those are the young lions that are roaring, pulling people away from a life of praise and trust in God. As we praise and trust Him for everything, then our prayers are answered.

But as the people of Judah listened to the young lions, they were devoured. They had laid waste his land, his towns are burned and deserted.

"Have you not brought this on yourself by forsaking the Lord your God when He led you in the way? " Jeremiah 2:17

Frequently couples find themselves stale and cold in their marriage, and stale and cold in their responsibility as the bride of Christ because they have listened to the young lions. They don't have that devotion of a youthful bride.

Consider this: what was the most exciting thing you did when you were just saved, when you had just accepted the Lord? Think about maybe the first person you told.

There was a little bit of trepidation, a little bit of holy fear as to how they would react, but inside you were compelled. You had to tell somebody what happened!

Because the enemy is defeated by the blood of the Lamb and the word of our testimony (Revelation 12:11), the roaring lion is trampled underfoot as we tell somebody what God has done. That living water, flowing from your innermost being, compelled you to share with somebody the goodness of the Lord. Yet God is saying, "You're not devoted to me like you were in your youth, when we first covenanted together. When you were a fresh, new bride you were excited about the honeymoon. You wanted to let me pick you up and take you over the threshold, but now..."

A young bride goes through struggles. Did you have challenges on your wedding day? Probably.

Why? Because there are young lions, demon powers roaring to try to get you started off on your trek through the wilderness, not on God's path but on another path -- toward destruction.

On our wedding day, I had a temperature. Curiously enough, immediately after the wedding, my temperature dropped and I was back to normal.

Other things went wrong. Molly was upset when they delivered the flowers. Her bouquet was wilted. The light colored flowers were browned at the edges and they were wilted as well. At the end of the wedding reception, when it was time to embark into the desert wilderness, she knew I had prepared for the transportation.

She knew we were going from Morningside Heights on the upper west side of Manhattan (N.Y.C.) to the Regency Hotel in midtown Manhattan. The Regency Hotel was the kind of hotel where they mow the carpets once a week. It's the kind of hotel where you just want to lay there forever in the plush towels. It's just a wonderful place.

Molly came out of the reception, and there was a horse and carriage. She expected a limo, but she got a horse and carriage. Sometimes, when you expect a great blessing from God, He can turn it around so that He can say that He loves you as His bride, so that He can draw you to Him with great appreciation.

Molly was surprised and thrilled. However, to get from the upper west side down to midtown, we had to cross through some unsavory neighborhoods.

There were drunks laying on the sidewalks with their Saturday wine, rubbing their eyes, shaking their heads, yelling, "Oh man, a horse!" They had some other expletives that describe the horse and all of a sudden our ride was becoming not so romantic.

We were going through that desert place (a tension filled, poverty stricken place) but then we pulled into Central Park onto a horse path with beautiful flowers. The ride became romantic again. Then we pulled out of Central Park and were stuck in traffic, and it was less romantic again.

That's the journey of life. Did we have a wonderful wedding night? Yes, we did because we stayed devoted. The bride stayed devoted to the servant leader that God had gifted her with. God is calling each one of us, as a part of the bride of Christ, to stay devoted to the servant leader, no matter what the desert wilderness experience brings. No matter what price. No matter what cost.

You're on the journey now. It's a fresh wilderness experience and every time God takes you through a wilderness, there's a promised land.

Sometimes we forget the destination. During forty years of meandering in the desert, the children of Israel forgot the destination. But when they got into the promised land, they were a devoted bride.

This rebuke by Jeremiah, is the first words of the young prophet. A few chapters later in Jeremiah 5:14, God promises him, *"I will make My words in your mouth a fire."* (NIV)

God is pleased with Jeremiah's faithfulness not to give into the seduction of philosophy, psychology, sociology or humanism but to preach the word of the Lord as He gave it to him.

God is well pleased with him.

If you speak the word of the Lord into your household and into your marriage, God's going to say, "I'm going to make your words like fire that will purify and burn away anything that doesn't need to be there."

GOD CALLS EACH BRIDE TO STAY DEVOTED TO THE SERVANT LEADER, NO MATTER WHAT THE DESERT WILDERNESS EXPERIENCE BRINGS

In his very first words, his very first sermon, imagine a young evangelist standing up before a full stadium, addressing the nation, he says, "I remember the devotion of your youth, how as a bride you loved me and followed me through the desert."

Immediately, in his first message, he begins in the prophetic. He begins in the gift of God that God has stirred up within him. When he's fanned that gift into flame, it changes a nation and leads in a revival.

When he talks about devotion, he's referring to Israel's history when they arrived in the Promised Land. God's people trusted in the Lord with such deep devotion. So intimate was the entire nation's relationship with the Lord that the nation was considered the Lord's wife. Let it be so in America! Let is be so that our nation would be considered the Lord's bride.

Instead, America has become a land of drought and darkness, a land where no one travels safely. Much like the Hebrew children, God has brought us into a fertile land to eat its fruit and rich produce. But we have defiled the land that God has given us by forsaking our devotion to Him, on which this nation was founded.

I wonder how many of us do that in our home. How many of us have forsaken the holy fear of God and pursued other gods?

Jeremiah added, "You have pursued other gods, by the way, they're not gods." He even had to clarify their idolatry for them. He said, "The leaders have rebelled against Me. The prophets prophesied byBaal."

The prophets today in America are speaking psychology as religion; they're speaking it to our children in the schools. That's their religion.

The New Age gurus are speaking philosophy to your co-workers. Every single one of the Fortune 100 companies in America has had a New Age seminar - every single one. The prophets the leaders of the land, are speaking by Baal, they're not speaking by the word of the Lord.

But don't despair! It just takes a few people to make a change. It just takes a few people to be totally devoted to Him. What price are you willing to pay to have God's love in your life? What price are you willing to pay? Take the time to join hands with your spouse and pray. Determine that you will be devoted to God, then watch Him bless you.

THE VALUE OF SUBMISSION

"Now it came to pass in the days of Ahasuerus (this was the Aha-suerus who reigned over one hundred and twenty seven provinces from India to Ethiopia), in those days when King Ahasuerus sat on the throne of his kingdom, which was in Shushan the citadel, that in the third year of his reign he made a feast for all his officials and servants - the powers of Persia and Media, the nobles, and the princes of the provinces being before him - when he showed the riches of his glorious kingdom and the splendor of his excellent majesty for many days, one hundred and eighty days in all." Esther 1:1-4

King Ahasuerus threw a party, a one hundred and eighty day party, a six-month party. King Ahasuerus had a wife named Vashti. She was a woman who had her own mind and moved in her own will. Usually I spend most of my time talking to men, but this topic is for women.

This will bring liberty for some women. Liberty is not the freedom to do what you like, but the freedom to do what you ought.

I Samuel 15:23 says, *"For rebellion is as the iniquity of witchcraft, and stubbornness is as sin and idolatry, because you have rejected the word of the Lord."*

We know rebellion is the natural state of woman. In Genesis 3:16, when God proclaimed the curse in the garden, He said, *"Your desire shall be for your husband"*. It had nothing to do with physical or sexual desire but it meant an ambition to usurp authority.

A woman's natural state is a desire to take away her husband's God given authority. The natural woman operates in rebellion.

The supernatural, or more than natural, woman rises above her sinful nature by the grace and help of God, to overcome rebellious tendencies. More on that later.

We're told rebellion is akin to witchcraft. That's a pretty strong statement.

Marijuana is to the drug culture what rebellion is to women's liberation. Most people who get involved in heavy drugs began with marijuana. It is an open door. Most women who get involved in the women's liberation movement begin in a state of rebellion.

Most people who get involved in the occult begin with Ouija or astrology or something that seems harmless. And it's that way with women. Women who begin in rebellion desire to be a part of the women's liberation movement. The Greek word "pharmacheon", which means sorcerer, or someone who uses something for the purpose of enchantment.

Most women use rebellion for the purpose of enchantment, trying to manipulate or govern over their husbands. Why? Because that's woman's natural state according to Genesis 3:16.

Let's look at how women can rise above the natural state and operate in the supernatural in order to be in submission to God's will and not be in rebellion. By defining the word "rebellion", most women can see where they've had at least moments of rebellion in the past week. I pray that by the end of this chapter that might change in the future.

We are flesh and we operate in rebellion, yet the Bible says rebellion is akin to witchcraft. If we look at the women's liberation movement, it has gained its authority through rebellion against any authority that's placed over women.

At a convention of the National Organization of Women, they came up with four resolutions:

1) Free abortions internationally upon demand to all women.

2) Continued expansion of school-based health clinics (SBCs). School based health clinics have expanded since 1979. These are clinics where presumably nurses teach young ladies about birth control. They do it under the guise of health care, but what they do is teach "safety" in sexual immorality.

3) Free birth control for all ages.

4) Full homosexual rights in schools, military and government. It is interesting that a feminist organization (the word "feminist" sounds so nice and feminine and harmless) would include full homosexual rights. What does that have to do with the dignity of a woman?

Yet this is part of what is rooted in rebellion. And unless each and every woman comes to grips with the fact that at times her nature is to rebel, then she won't be able to have victory over that rebellion.

Only when we face ourselves in the mirror of the Word of God, can we see what our human, fleshly and imperfect nature is. Then we can rise above that imperfect nature and apply the Word of God so that we don't live in that imperfect state.

God's condition for women, in the natural, is to be in rebellion at times, especially in the area of their husband's authority. That's what happened in the Garden of Eden as a result of sin.

Once we recognize that rebellion is part of what's messing up marriages today - it's just the natural flesh, not necessarily demonic — then we can deal with it.

Satan is out there and he wages war against marriage but a lot of what messes us up in marriage is our flesh: the husband's pride and ego, and often time, a woman's rebellion. Those are two basic root causes of a lot of marital problems.

The problem is that rebellion breeds this attitude in women that says, "Boy, women need more rights. Women should be more involved." Jesus was the greatest feminist who ever lived. He truly was interested in the dignity of a woman. He was the first of the Rabbinical priesthood to sit down and talk with women, eye to eye, in places He shouldn't have been talking to them.

He was the first to give women dignity in His ministry. The first to allow women to be around Him in the "inner circle" while He taught. He was the first to be a feminist by the pure meaning of feminist. He was interested in the dignity of a woman.

The word feminist today has very little to do with the dignity of a woman. Quite to the contrary, it removes the dignity of a woman and tries to blend the sexes. The word feminist today could be associated with the unisex movement. I've heard it said the latest thing in women's clothing is men's styling. I am disturbed when I go to a restaurant and the waitress is wearing a man's tie and shirt.

You may think that's a bit legalistic, but I'm not so much offended by the tie itself but by the concept that they are forcing a woman to appear like a man.

Sometimes people have that same trouble in their marital relationship. Men want the woman to appear as a man, so women rebel.

A woman isn't your buddy or sports partner. They can be your friend and everything else to you, but don't make them a man. Don't ask your wife to be a man, to take on responsibilities she's not suited for. Don't ask your wife to respond in a way that is contrary to her very being.

Learn who she is and how God created her and then honor her as that. Then you, like Jesus, will be giving your wife dignity.

Let's go back and look at a form of rebellion. The book of Esther teaches us what the effect of rebellion is.

Esther 1:9-11: *"Queen Vashti also made a feast for the women in the royal palace which belonged to King Ahasuerus. On the seventh day, when the heart of the king was merry with wine, he commanded... the seven eunuchs who served in the presence of the King Ahasuerus, to bring Queen Vashti before the king wearing her royal crown, in order to show her beauty to the people and the officials, for she was beautiful to behold."*

We know that Queen Vashti had a little bit of vanity in her. She refused to come at the king's command brought by the eunuchs.

"Therefore the king was furious, and his anger burned within him. Then the king said to the wise men who understood the times... "What shall we do to Queen Vashti, according to law, because she did not obey the command of King Ahasuerus brought to her by the eunuchs?"

THE WORD "FEMINIST" TODAY HAS VERY LITTLE TO DO WITH THE DIGNITY OF A WOMAN

And Memucan answered before the king and the princes: "Queen Vashti has not only wronged the king, but also all the princes, and all the people who are in all the provinces of King Ahasuerus. For the queen's behavior will become known to all women, so that they will despise their husbands in their eyes, when they report, "King Ahasuerus commanded Queen Vashti to be brought in before him but she did not come." This very day the noble ladies of Persia and Media will say to all the king's officials that they have heard of the behavior of the queen. Thus there will be excessive contempt and wrath." Esther 1:12-18

The rebellion of one woman can lead to the rebellion of many women. Rebellion breeds rebellion. That's why you have to chastise an unruly child, because he'll make other children unruly.

Rebellion breeds rebellion. You can't force obedience, but you need to discipline rebellion. Here we are told that Vashti's disobedience and rebellion would spread nationwide. The wise men of the land informed the king that her rebellion would spread nationwide unless it was nipped in the bud. Rebellion is like a wildfire.

Verses 19 and 20 shows an attempt by the wise men to legislate against rebellion. *"If it pleases the king, let a royal decree go out from him, and let it be recorded in the law of the Persians and the Medes, so that it shall not be altered, that Vashti shall come no more before King Ahasuerus, and let the king give her royal position to another who is better than she. When the king's decree which he will make is proclaimed throughout all his empire, (for it is great), all wives will honor their husbands, both great and small."* No way!

Just because the king decrees obedience doesn't mean obedience will occur. Here the wise men have gone wrong.

They think if the king decrees that Vashti can no longer come before him that will intimidate all the other women and they will honor their husbands both great and small. If you get a group of ladies together in a room and they find out one of their friends has been banished for one simple action, do you think all of a sudden they'll humbly obey everything the banisher says? No way!

THE REBELLION OF ONE WOMAN CAN LEAD TO THE REBELLION OF MANY WOMEN. REBELLION BREEDS REBELLION.

The wise men don't understand women at all. You can't dictate obedience. You can't legislate to those who are rebellious and have not placed themselves under authority.

Unless obedience is willful, it is not submission. Obedience that is not submission breeds resentment and contempt. In other words, if you force a child to obey but you don't teach them why they have to obey, they have no will in that obedience. They will resent the punishment without understanding the submission.

Submission is Willful

We need to operate in willful submission. We have to create an atmosphere whereby we can teach one another, communicate and talk to each other, willfully obey the Word of the Lord and be in willful submission. We can't dictate obedience. That was the mistake the wise men made here.

Our marriages are emblems of the bride of Christ. We must learn the value of mutual submission to the authority of Jesus Christ.

Then the king asked for all the beautiful young virgins to be prepared for him. He was going to pick another queen, so they prepare all these beautiful young virgins for his review.

Finally they come up with Esther. She is the cousin of Mordecai. She is an orphan girl. Her parents died and Mordecai raised her and brought her up. Mordecai was a great man of God.

He was not intimidated by anybody. He had the compassion to raise this orphan girl who turned out to be a beautiful girl. She was one of the virgins who was brought before the king.

We find out that she was beautiful and prepared to meet the king. When she was brought before Hagai, custodian of the women, she pleased him and obtained his favor. He set aside seven choice maidservants to be provided for her from the king's palace to make her beautiful.

I think King Ahasuerus had a major problem. All the maidservants brought in before him had to be prepared for a year before they were brought into the room to see him.

Six months of being rubbed with oil and six months of being perfumed. He wanted them to smell sweet and look fine.

When Esther went to the king she obtained the king's favor. However, Mordecai warns her not to reveal to the king that she's a Jewish girl, because he wouldn't appreciate it.

Mordecai, in his wisdom, warns her not to talk to her man about her in-laws. That's a good word of warning.

Sometimes a young lady becomes interested in a young man and they'll talk so much about their parents that they never learn who each other is. Perhaps they get married to find the parents' will is more important than their will. They never learn to be in willful submission, one to another, because they are intimidated by what their parents think of them.

Mordecai warned her to not talk to him about her parents. It was a good word of warning.

"Esther had not revealed her people or family for Mordecai had charged her not to reveal it. And everyday Mordecai paced in front of the court of the women's quarters, to learn of Esther 's welfare and what was happening to her." Esther 2: 10-1 1

Mordecai even cared for her when she was out of the sphere of his care. What's wrong with families today?

They operate in so much rebellion that once one child leaves the house, other brothers or sisters forget about their welfare.

Mordecai was so concerned that he stepped up and followed up and stayed right near her.

Esther 2:15: *"Now when the turn came for Esther the daughter of Abigail the uncle of Mordecai, who had taken her as his daughter, to go into the king, she requested nothing but what Hegai the king's eunuch, the custodian of the women, advised. And Esther obtained favor in the sight of all who saw her "*

Why? Because she requested nothing. Amazing. Later we'll see that Esther received up to half the kingdom. The king gave her half of everything he had. I believe she received that right at this moment because when she was brought before the king she requested nothing. She asked for nothing except what the king's servant had suggested.

She was even in submission to her servant and followed his instructions when she went to see the king. She asked for nothing and as a result she obtained favor from everyone who saw her.

Esther had to be a pretty awesome girl. She was so beautiful everyone was stunned by her beauty and she had a humble spirit. She didn't request anything. She just lived righteously. She checked with her cousin who had raised her about what the Word of the Lord would say and tell her to do.

A Submitted Life Obtains Favor

Esther lived a life of submission and obtained favor in the sight of all who saw her. It happens that King Ahasuerus then commands that everyone in the kingdom should bow before him on their knee and worship him. This man whom Esther is being hooked up to has a major ego problem.

First of all, he throws a one hundred and eighty day party.

Secondly, just because his wife wouldn't come to see him when he requested her, he banishes her from the kingdom.

King Ahasuerus elected Haman higher than that of any other noble. The king commanded that everyone kneel down to Haman. However, Mordecai doesn't bow down and worship him.

Mordecai was a Jew and he stated he would worship no one but his God. Mordecai stood up for his God when it wasn't popular to do so. Then there were consequences to pay. As a result, Haman got really angry with Mordecai.

But Mordecai had done something that had really given him favor with the king. Mordecai stood up for righteousness and he did the right thing in all circumstances.

WE MUST LEARN THE VALUE OF MUTUAL SUBMISSION TO THE AUTHORITY OF JESUS CHRIST

Previously he was sitting outside the king's gate, he discovered two guys were planning to kill the king. Mordecai came forth and told Esther of the assassination plot. They captured the two guys and executed them. The king's life was saved.

Even though this was a king of a reprobate mind, unrighteous, unfaithful and not a believer, Mordecai did the right thing and protected him. He prayed for those in authority over him, Mordecai was a man of God and he did the right thing.

The thing Mordecai had done came back to help him.

When you do things in righteousness, not in rebellion, they will come back to help you.

It would have been easy for Mordecai to have that spirit of rebellion and say, "Well, these guys are plotting to kill the king. The children of Israel might get set free as a result of this. Wow! I'd better let them kill him." That's what the spirit of rebellion would have said.

Instead Mordecai said, "No. He's the king who's been set in authority over us. I believe in God permitting authority. Someone is plotting to kill him. Murder is wrong. I'm going to report it so it will be taken care of."

I think it was because Mordecai walked in righteousness, that he had the constitution and strength to stand up and say, "No I'm not going to bow down to Haman. I've been in obedience so far, but once you ask me to worship someone else, besides God, that's where my obedience stops."

It is important to understand that it's not rebellion that Mordecai operated in. He was in total submission. His submission and obedience were first to the Lord and not to the king. So he operated in submission in that way.

Haman is furious about Mordecai not bowing to him. He comes to the king and says, "Hey, this Mordecai guy who's not bowing down in the courts, he's a Jew. I think we ought to kill all the Jews."

Haman says, " I will put up 10,000 talents of silver (the equivalent of over $4 billion today) to fund the extermination of the Jews."

Now you know this king who throws 180-day parties is motivated by materialism. So he thinks, "Sounds like a good deal to me. Four billion bucks to run my government and get rid of these people who are an annoyance and rebellious. Get rid of the whole lot of them. Go ahead and do it. In fact, Haman, I'm putting you in charge of my military. I'll make you a five-star general to exterminate the Jewish people."

Mordecai learns of this and is totally torn up. He struggles with it. He knows he did the right thing by not bowing down and worshipping Haman. He worshipped God and God alone. But all of a sudden he's burdened with the fact that his entire race may be exterminated because of his actions.

Therefore, he repents before the Lord. He thinks he's done wrong. This is what a holy man does. He examines himself in every situation. Mordecai gets rid of his clothes and clothes himself with sackcloth, a sign of repentance. Then he goes up as close as he can to the king's gate and cries out to the Lord.

Esther is horribly embarrassed by this. In fact, she sends out clothes with one of her maidservants to give to Mordecai.

Then all the Jewish people began to fast and weep wearing sackcloth. Mordecai's leadership, his holiness and righteousness, shone forth in such a way that the other people in their time of need looked to it.

It's amazing when people are in a time of crisis -when they face extermination — where do they turn? To government? Hollywood? No, they turn to God. The entire nation of Israel turned to God, crying out in sackcloth.

But Haman had his agenda. He's been sent from hell to exterminate the Jewish people. He says, "We'll kill them anyway." He tries to cover up all that's occurring from the king.

Esther 4:7-14: *"And Mordecai told him all that had happened to him, and the sum of money that Haman had promised to pay into the king's treasuries to destroy the Jews. He also gave him a copy of the written decree for their destruction, which was given at Shushan, that he might show it to Esther and explain it to her, and that he might command her to go in to the king to make supplication to him and plead before him for her people. So Hathach returned and told Esther the words of Mordecai.*

Then Esther spoke to Hathach, and gave him a command for Mordecai: "All the king's servants and the people of the king's provinces know that any man or woman who goes into the inner court to the king, who has not been called, he has but one law: put all to death, except the one to whom the king holds out the golden scepter, that he may live. Yet I myself have not been called to go in to the king these thirty days."

So they told Mordecai Esther's words.

And Mordecai told them to answer Esther. "Do not think in your heart that you will escape in the king's palace any more than all the other Jews. For if you remain completely silent at this time, relief and deliverance will arise for the Jews from another place, but you and your father's house will perish. Yet who knows whether you have come to the kingdom for such a time as this?"

IF YOU DON'T DO WHAT IS RIGHT, GOD WILL RAISE UP SOMEONE WHO WILL

Mordecai is more and more impressive as an example of willful submission to God. Here's Queen Esther, his cousin whom he raised in the palace. He tells her, "You're the one who can reach the king and change this decree to keep our people from being destroyed."

Fear comes upon her, and she worries, "I haven't been in the inner court to see the king for 30 days. Anyone who goes in there unannounced, unless he permits them to touch the scepter, is put to death. What should I do? I don't think Mordecai is using wisdom."

Mordecai answers her and tells her it doesn't matter. If you don't do it, God will raise someone else up to save our people. I believe sometimes God sends different anointing on different men and women of God because someone else didn't seize it. God will raise someone up to fill a void every single time.

Mordecai then issues a threat to his own cousin and says, "You think you're safe in the palace. They'll find out you're a Jew and you'll be exterminated too!"

Obedience is Life!

He uses the reality of fear to motivate her to do right. At this point, Esther understands that obedience is vital to her very existence.

I think this is the point where Esther realizes even though she has been a submissive person all her life, obedience to the will of God is what determines your survival.

Some ladies may struggle with rebellion toward their husband, but if they operate in obedience to the Word of the Lord all the time, their survival is guaranteed.

Whether your survival comes from one direction or another, it doesn't matter. God will raise someone up to bring your survival.

If you have financial pressures in your home and you think they are brought on by your spouse, do the will of the Lord and He will deliver you. He'll raise someone or something up and deliver you if you're in total obedience, even if you're in total obedience at the very point of extinction, such as bankrupcy or eviction. God will raise someone up to deliver you at that time.

Esther 5:1-2 *"Now it happened on the third day that Esther put on her royal robes and stood in the inner court of the king's palace, across from the king's house, while the king sat on his royal throne in the royal house, facing the entrance of the house. So it was, when the king saw Queen Esther standing in the court, that she found favor in his sight, and the king held out to*

Esther the golden scepter that was in his hand. Then Esther went near and touched the top of the scepter"

What a symbol that the king saw her and now she was robed in righteousness. Now she was robed in the will of God. Now he was going to be used to complete the will of the Lord. Even though the king was unfaithful, without saying a word, couldn't help but obey the Spirit of God on him.

He reached out his scepter so she could touch it. She would not be put to death -- she had entrance to come into the inner court of the king.

It's amazing how God will create favor. Consistently, Esther had favor in the king's sight, favor in the sight of all who saw her.

Obedience Opens the Door to Favor

I believe Esther learned to pray for favor and as a result, doors were open to her. Ladies, if you'll pray for favor with your husband, there will be fewer times you'll be tempted to operate in rebellion. You will have a trust in God's will in your life and that God's favor will be there for you when you need it with your husband. You won't have to take things into your own hands and try to create a rebellious attitude where you control the situation. This is a powerful truth.

"And the king said to her, "What do you wish, Queen Esther? What is your request? It shall be given to you - up to half the kingdom!" Esther 5:3

Awesome! All of a sudden the king, with all of his different wives and earthly possessions, at Esther's very appearance gives her half of the kingdom, because she's obeyed the will of the Lord.

Do you know what the symbol of that is in marriage? The two becoming one. She now gets half because she's not in rebellion, but in submission to the will of the Lord. She's not necessarily in submission to her husband. But she's in submission to the will of the Lord first.

If she's in the will of the Lord, then she'll be in submission to her husband if her husband is serving God. King Ahasuerus was not serving God. She was still submissive to him in attitude, but her first submission was to God. As a result, God gives her half the kingdom, even before she asks.

Ahasuerus is so overcome by her beauty and the presence of the Lord upon her he asks for her request and gives it to her.

"If it pleases the king, let the king and Haman come today to the banquet that I have prepared for him."

Then the king said, "Bring Haman quickly, that he may do as Esther has said." So the king and Haman went to the banquet that Esther had prepared.

At the banquet of wine the king said to Esther, "What is your petition? It shall be granted you. What is your request, up to half the kingdom? It shall be done! "

Then Esther answered and said, "My petition and request is this:

If I have found favor in the sight of the king (Boy, she's a great saleswoman, too) *and if it pleases the king to grant my petition and fulfill my request, then let the king and Haman come to the banquet which I will prepare for them, and tomorrow I will do as the king has said"* Esther 5:4-8

Amazing! Even at a time of great favor she doesn't ask for the full request. She waits upon the Lord, and she perseveres. Her patience shows her submission. The king is not threatened as if she came to manipulate him. She just came to have another banquet.

WHEN YOU DO RIGHT YOU WILL GET YOUR JUST RECOMPENSE, DOING RIGHT HAS ITS OWN REWARD.

We know that the entire nation of Israel is saved as a result of her finally coming to a point where she can say to the king "Let my people go. Let the Jewish people go."

In the next chapter the king is troubled and can't sleep. In order to fall asleep, he calls and asks to have the record of the chronicles read to him. He wants to know what's been happening in his kingdom.

One of the events read to him was the plot to kill the king that Mordecai overheard. Instead of the king being killed, the assassins were arrested and put to death.

Then the king asks, "Who is this guy Mordecai? Why hasn't he been rewarded for this?"

Mordecai's righteousness has again come back to bless him a second time. Your righteousness will serve you. Your righteousness in God's sight will serve you. When you do right you will get your recompense. Doing right has its own reward. Every time you do right there is a reward attached to it. The reward may come now or later but it will come.

That reward saved Mordecai at the very time Haman was planning to kill him because Mordecai was the leader of this "rebellion". But Mordecai was not the leader of the rebellion but instead was in submission to the will of God. That's why his righteousness stood up.

You might find yourself in a situation where you don't want to do the right thing with your spouse. You might not want to love them when you know it's tough to do so. But that's when you have to do it all the more.

Your righteousness will have its reward but the rebellion is akin to witchcraft. The rebellion will bring evil back to you like witchcraft.

Are you beautiful before the king? Not just for your husband, but for the King of Kings? Are there moments when your spouse makes you angry and just for that moment you rebel against God by not doing the will of God? We can't let the provocation of our spouse lead us into unrighteousness, but we must choose to walk in love.

THREE STEPS TO A DELIGHTFUL MARRIAGE

Often God ministers to us in threes. In marriage there is a paradigm to help us fully understand that He ministers in threes. We deal with our spirit, our flesh and our mind. Those three things are what we are made up of.

If we put the emphasis on the spirit we'll put less emphasis on the body and we'll be in balance according to God's Word. Many times couples have great expectations for their marriage.

Here's what every woman expects and would like her husband to be:

-a brilliant conversationalist, sensitive, kind, understanding, truly loving and very hard working,

- helps around the house by washing dishes, vacuuming floors and taking care of the yard,

- helps her raise the children,
- emotionally and physically strong,
- as smart as Einstein but who looks like Brad Pitt.

Here's what she gets:

- A husband who always takes her to the best restaurants, some day he may even take her inside.

- He doesn't have any ulcers. He gives them.

-Anytime he gets an idea in his head he gets the whole thing in a nutshell.

- He's a well-known miracle worker - it's a miracle when he works.

- He supports his wife in the manner in which she is accustomed to being supported - he lets her keep her job.

- He's such a bore he even bores her to death when he gives her a compliment.

- His occasional flashes of silence make his conversation brilliant.

Let's look at the other side of the coin. What does a husband expect from an ideal wife?

- A lot of times a man would like a woman who's always beautiful and cheerful.

- She could have married a movie star but wanted only him.

- She has hair that never needs curlers or beauty shops.

- She has beauty that won't run in a rainstorm.

- She's never sick - just allergic to jewelry.

- She insists that moving furniture by herself is good for her figure.

- She's an expert at cooking, cleaning the house, fixing the car or TV, painting the house and keeping quiet.

- Her favorite hobbies include mowing the lawn and ironing.

- She hates charge cards and her favorite expression is, "What can I do for you dear?"

- Finally she loves you because you're sexy.

But what most men get is:

- a woman who speaks 140 words per minute with gusts up to 180.

- She was once a model for a totem pole.

- She's a light eater. As soon as it gets light, she starts eating.

- Where there's smoke there she is - cooking.

- She lets you know you have only two faults, everything you say and everything you do.

-No matter what she does with it, her hair looks like an explosion in a steel wool factory.

- If you get lost all you have to do is open your wallet she'll find you.

Often times we have different expectations than what we receive in our marriage.

Romans 8:8,14 says, *"So then, those who are in the flesh cannot please God."* ... *"For as many as are led by the Spirit of God, these are sons of God."*

Usually at the start of marriage we see areas where we differ. We can differ in many different areas, but the Lord has been dealing with me with this system of threes.

In counseling I find the three areas that come up more than any others are conflict, selfishness and dishonesty. I think all of us have engaged in these areas in our marriage.

Conflict in the spirit can be healthy. You can grow through conflict in the spirit. But conflict in the flesh is contrary.

Selfishness hurts, and dishonesty hurts.

Dishonesty is an area where many Christians are slow to confess. It's something the enemy attacks us with all the time, little areas of dishonesty in our marriage.

OUR EXPECTATIONS IN MARRIAGE OFTEN DIFFER FROM WHAT WE ACTUALLY RECEIVE IN THE RELATIONSHIP

Maybe it's a little white lie of convenience or the thing you don't tell your spouse that you know you need to tell them, as the Holy Spirit has dealt with you. Those areas of dishonesty bring division.

We have these divisions because of how our very human nature is. With sin came shame, dishonesty, fear, and anger. Man was no longer naked and innocent but he was clothed and covered.

The goal of a great marriage is to be naked and innocent with your spouse: being transparent and vulnerable. It is the type of nakedness where dishonesty can't come in and where selfishness is set aside. If you have that then you can go back to that vertical relationship with God and you live a pure life.

Instead of living each day in unhindered fellowship with our creator, sin enters in and we hide from Him and question His love for us, knowing our love for Him is imperfect.

WE QUESTION OUR SPOUSE'S LOVE FOR US BECAUSE WE KNOW OUR LOVE FOR THEM IS IMPERFECT

Our relationship with our spouse is not right if dishonesty, selfishness, or carnal conflict creeps in. What we then do is to hide ourselves from our spouse.

We question our spouse's love for us because we know our love for them is imperfect. Our vertical relationship with God has a lot to do with our horizontal relationship with our spouse.

You might ask each other the following questions in a different way: "How am I doing?" That's a question that creates a lot of conflict.

"How do I look?" I'm not talking about physical appearance but how do I appear, what's my image? That often motivates selfishness.

"How important am I?" We all seek to be important. How important am I is a question that leads to honesty or dishonesty.

If we recognize that we're really unimportant in and of ourselves, that we can do nothing apart from Jesus, then we're not worried about how important we are.

But if we're worried about how important we are that's when the temptation for dishonesty will creep in.

Conflict says, how am I doing? That's where the spirit of competitiveness and contrariness comes in.

How am I doing? You want to be competitive against your spouse.

How do I look? Selfishness.

How do I appear to others? I'm concerned about how I look, not how we look as a couple. Not how my spouse looks. Am I preferring my spouse before myself? But how do I look? That's where selfishness comes in.

Then, "How important am I?"

Performance motivates conflicts. If we're driven by performance we want that competitiveness, that winning attitude, to engage in conflict. You like the war, the sporting event, the event that pits you against someone else so that you have the opportunity to win.

Selfishness often has to do with position and how we view our position.

Dishonesty often has to do with possession and what we own or want to own, even if it's a feeling. Maybe that dishonesty is motivated by wanting your spouse's love, so you don't tell something to your spouse that would create an area of discomfort. You don't want to lose that possession of your spouse's love. You're afraid you might lose your spouse's love.

So we have performance, position and possession.

Conflict	Selfishness	Dishonesty
Performance	Position	Possession

Interestingly, these were all perfect in the garden, before the fall. Adam had performance in dominion over everything.

He had position and status. A lot of men are looking for status. And that drives men's selfishness.

Adam had possession. He owned everything. He had all that he needed. He owned everything he could have desired; yet that was not enough. His relationship was lacking.

Another way you can relate to these three is as areas of spiritual attack in our lives.

If conflict is an area, what area of your spiritual life does conflict attack? It attacks your fellowship. Your ability to communicate and commune with your spouse is what conflict attacks. It's an attack on your fellowship.

Then selfishness interferes. What area of your marriage is selfishness most evident in and most dangerous in?

Where do you have to put selfishness aside most in order to be successful in your marriage? In the flesh part of your relationship. The sexual and physical relationship is the area we tend to want to be most selfish. Most people are interested in their own physical pleasure in lovemaking. But spiritually, if we set aside that selfishness then our flesh is in balance.

Dishonesty could come in finances. I think it's interesting to see that we have areas in common with each other and how the enemy would attack us in each of those areas. Dishonesty is often tied into finances.

There are a lot of people who give to the work of the Lord for tax reasons. I think God looks at our motive, our heart. God loves a cheerful giver. I'm not saying you shouldn't use the tax law. I believe you should take advantage of the law to the fullest extent within the law and the government shouldn't get any more than is absolutely necessary. We should try to get every tax advantage and benefit we can.

But if that's your motivation to giving to the Lord's work then that's dishonest. You're not being a cheerful giver, or paying tithes and offerings in love. You're paying in barter. You're hoping to get the tax benefit. If you give out of cheerfulness, obedience and love for God then He will free you up in your finances. This is an area that dishonesty creeps in and opens up the door to other areas of dishonesty.

Satan would like to rob us of the ability to prosper financially because then we can bless the work of God further. If we bless the work of God further then we'll have enough to bless our children with an inheritance.

This is one of the major reasons for divorce. Divorce decimates people financially. They end up paying child support here and child support there. Spouses who are used to an income suddenly don't have an income and have to pursue another source of income.

It's one of the reasons Satan loves divorce; he can mess people up financially. Then he can hinder God's plan to bless the work of God while he is impeding the plan of God for a loving family to bless their children with an inheritance. If you raise up a godly child who knows what to do with his/her finances and he receives an inheritance, that's even more potent against the kingdom of darkness and for the Kingdom of God. Finances have a lot to do with our dishonesty as well. Some of these areas will overlap into others. But in general you can see a pattern here, a pattern of attack.

Conflict	Selfishness	Dishonesty
Performance	Position	Possession
Fellowship	Flesh	Finances

There are basically three areas that motivate us in our lives.

One is our emotion, our feeling.

One is our will or desire.

The other is our mind or thought pattern.

Each one is related to one of the previously men¬tioned areas of vulnerability. For example, conflict usual¬ly has to do with our emotions. If you can control your emotions and feelings, generally speaking, you won't get into carnal or fleshly conflict. You'll be able to operate in the fruit of the Spirit that is self-control. You won't be motivated by that feeling of wanting to get your spouse back or the one-up feeling - the feeling of wanting to win an argument.

If we control our will, it is the center of our desire.

If we control our desire sexually, then we'll be able to give our spouse the gift of God that is in lovemaking.

If we control ourselves in the pursuit of position and status we'll be able to humble ourselves and let the Lord lift us up.

If we control our will or desire about how we look, and not be so concerned about it, but instead be concerned about how others around us look, we can get a lot more accomplished. We won't be as concerned over who gets the credit but that the job gets done.

If we control our will and desire and put aside selfishness and die to self then we can see true life, and be richly blessed.

The third area is the mind or thought pattern. That's why dishonesty is usually rooted in the mind. Lies grow out of our thought life.

"For as he thinketh in his heart, so is he." Proverbs 23:7 KJV

Sometimes dishonesty creeps down into your heart and all of a sudden gets into your mind and you get an idea like, "Boy, if I just don't say that, it could make life easier." Dishonesty creeps in.

Our mind has more to do with our finances than does our desire or emotions.

You might say, "Oh I don't know. I feel like I really need those things. I want those things. It's a feeling I have."

FAITH BECOMES REAL WHEN YOU GET PAST MERE REASON INTO THE REALITY OF REVELATION

No, that's a thought you have. The thought grows into a feeling because you've allowed your will and desire to give in to that feeling. Most materialism is bred first in thought. You accept a thought or image through television advertising or seeing something your neighbor has, and think that you need to be at that same level. You want to receive the same form of materialism. It begins with a thought.

How important am I? That's a thought. In your heart of hearts, in the purity of your emotions, how important you are doesn't matter. It's a comparison based on levels, part of your thought life.

What you own or what you possess is more important in your mind than in actuality. Why can a missionary in the jungles of Africa be more content than someone living in a mansion? Because what that missionary possesses spiritually is more important than what he possesses materially.

What you possess spiritually is in spirit not in your mind. That's the difference. A lot of you try to walk out your Christianity in your mind and in your thought life and not in your spirit being. If you intellectualize your

Christianity you can go a long way — reason can go a long way.

There are some great Bible teachers that know the Word of God and teach purely on reason. But when you get past reason into revelation (where God reveals to you) then it becomes real in your own life.

Revelation occurs from God's Spirit to your spirit. Reason occurs in your mind. You can reason away the Gospel. There have been some great books for the logical and intellectual mind that will convince people of the veracity of Jesus Christ.

But unless a man receives Jesus in spirit he won't be born again. Reason can go a long way to helping someone understand. Your mind can go a long way to developing great finances, possessions, importance and even honesty, if you control your mind.

However, if you develop your mind devoid of your spirit it's going to be a ground where you might stumble.

Self-Control Is More than a Decision

Your emotions can be wonderful if you allow your spirit and heart to control them as opposed to your mind and your feelings. If you allow just your feelings to control your emotions you don't have any real self-control. That's why self-control is a fruit of the Spirit. When you allow self-control as a fruit of the Holy Spirit to control your emotions then your emotions will be pleasant.

That's not to say unpleasant things won't happen. But when unpleasant things happen, you'll control your emotions and understand where your feelings are coming from, what your feelings should be and how your feelings should line up with the Word of God.

If your spirit is not controlling your emotions, then you'll be beset by reacting to your own neurological impulses. Some people who have chemical imbalances are diagnosed manic-depressive. They ride up and down, and up and down, because they are reacting to their feelings. But I've seen people who are diagnosed as manic-depressive on heavy drugs be set free as the Spirit of God was born in them. They become balanced because now their spirit takes hold of their emotions. They're not living according to their emotions.

One of the strongest areas to attempt to control is the will. It's the will that controls our desire. If you have a desire to be in the flesh, you'll be in the flesh. If you have a desire to be in the spirit, you'll be in the spirit. Yet oftentimes we don't think of our will as being something that's conscious. Our will is both conscious and subconscious.

When our will is conscious, it's something we determine, we know and we move ourselves toward.

When our will is subconscious, it is something that has been received and accepted by us but we are not necessarily aware of at that time.

The will is powerful — both consciously and subconsciously. Sometimes the subconscious will is more powerful than the conscious will.

That's why the Bible warns against hypnotism. If you've ever been hypnotized you need to renounce that and pray against it.

Leviticus warns us we should not give our mind over to another. In hypnotism, another is planting thoughts into your subconscious mind and trying to get control of your will and desires subconsciously.

Some people try to quit smoking through hypnotism.

They're trying to place that will and desire into the subconscious. God knows that when you give over your will and your desire to someone else, then your spirit won't be able to control your will or desire.

THE WILL IS POWERFUL BOTH CONSCIOUSLY AND SUBCONSCIOUSLY. SOMETIMES THE SUBCONSCIOUS WILL IS MORE POWERFUL THAN THE CONSCIOUS WILL.

God desires His Holy Spirit to communicate with our spirit so that our spirit gives us the will and desire that lines up with God's will and God's desire.

We can look at this and then relate it to marriage and ask, what is the answer? How do we overcome all these areas and how do we make sure they are spiritual?

Jesus had a way. He said it in John 14:6: *"I am the way, the truth, and the life."*

"The way" includes our emotions, our fellowship, our performance, "how am I doing?" and how we deal with conflict. That's the way.

The way of Jesus is the way of peace. He is the Prince of Peace.

If you have the peace of Jesus, then you won't have conflict in the flesh. If you have the peace of Jesus, you won't ask, "How am I doing?" because you're doing it according to the Lord.

If you have the way of how to perform then your performance is not based on what you can do but on what Christ can do through you - *"I can do all things through Christ who strengthens me."* Philippians 4:13

If you have the way and peace, then your fellowship will be peaceful and your communications with others will be what God would have you to do.

If you have the way, then your emotions will line up with what God wants you to feel, then you can be led by the Spirit of God.

SPIRITUAL ATTACK

Conflict	Selfishness	Dishonesty
Performance	Position	Possession
Fellowship	Flesh	Finances
Emotions	Desires	Thoughts

• •

The Way	The Life	The Truth

JESUS

If you have the life that Jesus is speaking about, He wants you to *have life and life more abundantly* (John 10:10). We want the abundant life; our will and our desire is not as important when we pursue the abundant life. Selfishness subsides and is put down because we're having an abundant life being led by the Spirit of God, and our will is not as important.

Our flesh, or physical and sexual relationship can now become a spiritual thing because God desires us to have life and life more abundantly. He wants you to have a great sexual relationship with your spouse.

If you have that life more abundantly, then your position is not important. You won't get hung up about your position in life. No matter what your position in life, if you're enjoying life and life abundantly, knowing that you will have life eternally, then wherever you're at right now doesn't matter as much. Your position is not as important as it was if you're dealing in the flesh.

If you have life abundantly you're not concerned about how you look. You know you're looking right in the eyes of God. That's the only way you should be concerned about what you look like is that you look right in the eyes of God. Then selfishness is put aside. Why would we be selfish if we've already got life and life abundantly? If we have life abundantly then we want to give that out and help others to find life and life more abundantly.

Truth Frees the Mind

Then Jesus said He is the truth. If we have the truth of God we don't have to worry so much about our mind because we're *no longer conformed to this world, but we're transformed by the renewing of our mind* (Romans 12:2). What renews our mind is the Truth of God. So we're no longer conformed to everything the world does.

We're not conformed to dishonesty. We have Truth in us and we speak Truth, operate under Truth and are led by Truth so that dishonesty becomes less and less evident in our lives. That's why it's a constant and continual process in our lives when we undergo the renewal of our mind by the transforming power of the Word of God who is the Truth. Jesus is the way, the truth and the life and He is the Word made flesh. The Word of God is the Truth of our lives. So if we get that Truth in us then we don't have to worry about our mind.

The only thing I have to worry about is what am I putting in my mind, Truth or dishonesty? That's why I've got to spend more time in prayer and in the Word. If I want to have the way, peace and life I need to have that Truth in me so I can operate in the Truth.

Then I'm not concerned about my finances. If I have the Truth and I am a servant of the Lord Jesus Christ, it's incumbent upon the Master to take care of His servant. And He does so for us divinely — over and over and over again.

The Truth of God is that I'm to be a steward of what He gives me so then He blesses me in return. I've learned that debt is not of God. If we're to be conformed in the likeness of Him and He's a debtor to no man then we should be a debtor to no man. Once we get those principles of Truth in us then we live in those Truths and we are blessed.

IF WE HAVE LIFE ABUNDANTLY THEN WE WANT TO GIVE THAT OUT AND HELP OTHERS TO FIND LIFE AND LIFE MORE ABUNDANTLY

Then possessions don't matter. I like things - clothes and other possessions. But I know that those possessions don't give me any greater significance. The Truth is that I use those possessions so I might not be a stumbling block to someone else. If I came out to preach with a heavy metal rock T-shirt, it might be a stumbling block to some. They might be diverted from listening to the message.

But if we deal in the Truth we realize that without God we are nothing; we can do nothing and we have no life. In Him there is life, we have our very being and we live and move. Truth tells us we don't have to worry about how important we are. Then we deal on a level of honesty. All these things come together as we encompass Jesus.

In Romans chapter 8 one can see how this all relates to marriage and how these principles can be put into practice.

Verse 1 and 2: *"There is therefore now no condemnation to those who are in Christ Jesus, who do not walk according to the flesh, but according to the Spirit. For the law of the Spirit of life in Christ Jesus has made me free from the law of sin and death.*"

Many people continue to carry and still deal with that shame and guilt that Adam had in the garden because they are not walking in the law of the Spirit, in grace. They are not receiving God's love for them.

You can only love Jesus as much as you understand His love for you. His love bought us above the law of sin and death and gave us the law of the Spirit of righteousness and peace. That's tremendous that He would offer Himself that way.

Verse 3 and 4: "*For what the law could not do in that it was weak through the flesh, God did by sending His own Son in the likeness of sinful flesh, on account of sin: He condemned sin in the flesh, that the righteous requirement of the law might be fulfilled in us who do not walk according to the flesh but according to the Spirit.*"

That's the third time in four verses He says, not according to the flesh but according to the Spirit. Here it is again in verse 5, "*For those who live according to the flesh set their minds on the things of the flesh, but those who live according to the Spirit, the things of the Spirit.*"

If we want Truth, we've got to set our mind on the things of the Spirit and Truth, not on flesh. If we walk according to the flesh we're not going to have life but death.

Verse 6: "*For to be carnally minded is death, but to be spiritually minded is life and peace.*"

To be carnally minded, in the flesh, is death. To be spiritually minded is life and peace. It works out if we walk in the spirit and not in the flesh.

The carnal mind is enmity against God. Our old fleshly mind reacts against God. It has almost a built-in disrespect for God. A built-in misunderstanding, discomfort and concept that God would want to condemn us. But there is no condemnation to those who are in Christ Jesus.

"*So then, those who are in the flesh cannot please God.*" Romans 8:8.

You might want to put that up on your refrigerator or dashboard. That's a powerful verse. If we concentrate and meditate on that verse for some time we will be motivated to attempt to walk in the Spirit, not in the flesh. We cannot please God if we're walking in the flesh.

Verse 9: *"But you are not in the flesh but in the Spirit, if indeed the Spirit of God dwells in you. Now if anyone does not have the Spirit of Christ, he is not His."*

If the Spirit of Christ doesn't dwell in you, you will be bound and chained and fettered and held up by all these areas of attack in your life and in your marriage. Your marriage may be stymied by areas of bondage that you've chained yourself to because you haven't crossed over into the Spirit of Christ and allowed His Spirit to become preeminent in your life.

Verse 10 and 11: *"And if Christ is in you, the body is dead because of sin, but the Spirit is life because of righteousness.*

But if the Spirit of Him who raised Jesus from the dead dwell in you, He who raised Christ from the dead will also give life to your mortal bodies through His Spirit who dwells in you."

Here's the explanation of dying to self. A lot of people say if I die to self then I set my own needs aside. But He's saying here if the Spirit of Him who raised Jesus from the dead dwells in you, He who raised Christ from the dead will also give life to your mortal bodies through His Spirit.

OFTEN WE DON'T TAKE THE TIME TO PONDER OR THINK ABOUT WHAT WE DESIRE FOR OUR MARRIAGE

What He's saying is we've got the priority wrong. We put the body first, the mind second and then the spirit. But He says if we prioritize spirit first, mind second, and body third then that spirit will feed your body and mind. It will give life to the other areas of your being. But if we put our mind first then we won't have life but we'll have death. Also, if we put our body first then we won't have life but death. If we put our spirit first by the Spirit of God we are guaranteed life in body, mind and spirit.

Ask yourself what area in your life do you need to turn over to the Spirit of God? What area do you need the Spirit of God to lead in rather than being led by the flesh?"

The flesh might be the will, even the subconscious will. It might even be the will of the past, something you learned from your parents.

When someone says a harsh thing you react with the flesh. That's part of the subconscious will. This might be an area you need to arrest, and say, "Spirit of God I need you to help me to take control of my will that I might have gentleness, meekness and the other fruits of the Spirit."

Maybe you are performance driven. You get your significance from what you do. Find out who you are. Find the way of peace. Then what you do will be pleasant and effortless. Oftentimes those driven by performance and work (once they find the way of peace), become much more productive, efficient and effective.

If you're concerned with how you look or with your position and status, find out what life is, and life more abundantly. Find out what life in the Spirit is, with your spouse.

Get the truth of God in your life so you don't have to rely on the life you receive from other people's compliments. You don't receive life from your husband's compliments, or from someone desiring your flesh.

Maybe you spend all your time getting dolled up for yourself, so you can look in the mirror and say, "Boy I look good." That's selfishness. That's not life. Life more abundantly is to be able to stand in front of the mirror buck-naked thanking God for every piece of your body and saying, "God, I am your creation. You knew me before I was in my mother's womb. I thank you this is me. Maybe there are parts of me I can change, but this is me. I thank you for my life."

Choose to Walk in the Spirit

There are so many others who would like to have the life you have. Yet selfishness would keep you from living in thanksgiving of understanding life and life more abundantly.

Maybe you haven't found the Truth of God - that you're an overcomer, even more than a conqueror. You can do all things through Christ who strengthens you.

These principles work if you embrace the way of the Spirit. Walking out these principles on a daily basis will lead you to a great marriage. Make a decision. Try it and see!

Remember that God often works in threes. After all, He Himself is Three in One: the Father, Son and Holy Spirit.

As we learn by the Spirit to deal with the spiritual threes discussed thus far in this chapter, we must balance our lives with three practical steps that will help make your marriage a delight.

I Thessalonians 2:17 says, *"But we, brethren, having been taken away from you for a short time in presence, not in heart, endeavored more eagerly to see your face with great desire."*

The apostle Paul is saying that, even though he had not seen them for a little bit, he has been with them in heart, but still had a great desire to see them face-to-face.

The three steps to a delightful marriage begin here with what the apostle Paul is saying. You've got to have a great desire.

If I were to ask you to write in a sentence or two what is the desire for your marriage you might say: "I desire that we make it through next week." "I desire that we live in peace and harmony." "We have a great marriage but I desire that we do better with our children." Or "We are just learning about marriage but our desire is that we grow together spiritually."

The first point in having a delightful marriage is desire. Everything begins with desire. My question to you is, "What do you desire? Have you thought about that?"

Webster defines desire as to wish or long for, to crave or to want. What do you crave? Or do you crave anything?

Many marriages go from week to week, or from step to step, rather than living and planning and thinking and dreaming. It's because they don't have a desire. They don't know what their desire for their marriage is.

Desire begins all progress. I once heard it said in a business seminar that discontent is the beginning of all progress. I used to agree with that statement, but I disagree with it now. I believe desire is the beginning of all progress, because you can have a desire (which may be generated by discontent) that will cause you to progress.

Desire is one of the basic motivating forces in life. Often we don't take the time to ponder and think about what we desire for our marriage. What would make your marriage a delight?

We all have a desire for something. We all desire to be loved and respected for what we really are. And what are we? We're well meaning but imperfect. In other words, we all desire to be loved and respected but deep down we are all imperfect including our spouse. If we can understand that about our spouse then we can recognize that we need to have a desire to have a greater marriage than we have now.

We're all imperfect but we're all on that path of growing in God and attaining perfection so that we can be better than we are now. So the first step to a delightful marriage is desire.

The second step is discipline. Once you have the desire then you must take steps to make it occur. We must discipline ourselves daily. There are people who have much talent but let it go to waste because they are too lazy to discipline themselves. There are others who have less talent but still become great because they are willing to subject themselves daily to discipline.

We must train ourselves to excel. Webster defines discipline as training to act in accordance with rules. In terms of your marriage, what training are you going to act on in accordance with rules that you've set? If you don't communicate with your spouse about a common desire for your marriage (what you want to improve) then you don't know what steps of training to take.

Webster also defines discipline as instruction and exercise designed to train to proper conduct or action.

Are you receiving instruction? Are you exercising and putting into practice the principles God has shown you through His Word, prayer and teaching? Discipline takes responsibility.

As Christians we have a responsibility to others but we are also responsible for ourselves. In the world's view, legally most people are only responsible for themselves. What makes America different from other countries is that our founding fathers created a constitution that would make people responsible to others in a Christian way of thinking. That's what the Bill of Rights was about as well as the Declaration of Independence and the Constitution - making people responsible to others. In most other nations you are not responsible to others, only to the government.

But here we have an intrinsic right that allows us to pursue happiness until we infringe on the rights of others. And that's the Christian principle where we have a responsibility to other people. Unless you exercise that responsibility you lead an undisciplined life.

In fact, most Christians who have trouble disciplining themselves for daily events are people who live selfishly because they don't take the responsibility to others seriously. They may take responsibility for themselves, attempting to lead a righteous life, but the Christian life is morethan responsibility for ourselves. It's a responsibility to others.

IN MARRIAGE, ONE MUST GET BEYOND SELFISHNESS

Indeed, that is what Christ's discipline is all about. The discipline of Jesus Christ must be the mark of His disciples.

Think of someone who is the most awesome Christian you know. I love Pastor Tommy Barnett. He has such a disciplined life. He's disciplined to others - always courteous, kind and has the mark of the discipline of Christ. That's the mark of a true disciple - that mark of discipline.

The first level of Jesus' discipline is to get beyond selfishness. Many marriages suffer in this area. In order to discipline ourselves we have to get beyond selfishness. People can operate day in and day out being kind to others, being courteous on the job. Until they get home and they want their needs met. They want self first.

But yet that discipline of Christ-like love goes beyond the workplace, beyond the facade of day-to-day living and goes to the most vulnerable relationship of marriage.

In marriage one must get beyond selfishness. Florence Nightingale clothed the British army. She changed hospitals and the nursing profession forever. But she didn't do it the way most people would think. Most people think of her as this sweet little lady that cared for hurting people so gingerly.

Not so. Books written about her declare it was due to strict methods, stern discipline, ceaseless labor and a fixed determination of an indomitable will that allowed her to accomplish everything she set her hands to do. She was a very intense and focused person. Yes, she was kind and considerate but she wasn't just a sweet pushover.

She had a fixed purpose, a desire and she put ceaseless labor toward it. There was a strict method and she was stern in her discipline. Beneath her cool and calm demeanor there lurked fierce and passionate fire.

Put Discipline Toward Desire

Desire was implemented through discipline. You can have the greatest desire you want but if you never get out and practice what you desire, it won't make any impact on your life. Whatever you desire, you must put discipline toward it.

I desire to be a great prayer warrior. I have a good prayer life but I have a long, long way to go so I must discipline myself to pray even when I don't want to pray. Most people don't feel like praying all the time, so we must discipline ourselves at times when we don't want to.

Discipline has such great rewards. Some of you want to correct your spouse but you have no right to point out a lack of discipline in your spouse until you discipline your own life. Disciplining our lives is a lifelong process.

My wife is a free moral agent. She has a relationship with God that is separate from mine. We have a relationship with God together but she has a separate relationship with God as well. I must allow her room to grow there and if I believe in the power of prayer and intercession then I've got to intercede for her to grow.

If she believes in the power of intercession then she must pray for me, rather than correcting all the time. Some of you are challenged by the fact that you are corrected by your spouse all the time. I don't want to take that doctrine too far to say your spouse should never correct you. Some of you will say to your spouse "See you should never correct me." No. We should also be gracious and learn to receive correction from our spouse.

I must be humble before the Lord. My ability to correct my wife about a lack of discipline in any area of her life is related directly to how disciplined I am in that area of my life. That's a pure and humble way of coming before the Lord and examining myself before I attempt to dictate other issues.

Psalms 50:16,17 says, *"But to the wicked God says: 'What right have you to declare My statutes, or take My covenant in your mouth, seeing you hate instruction and cast My Words behind you?'"*

If you hate the Lord's discipline or hate instruction and cast the Words of the Lord behind you, you can come to church and someone can preach a dynamic message about a specific area, but if it doesn't reach you or if you hear it and then you cast those words behind you, you have no right the Lord says to talk about what He says or to take His covenant on your lips!

Deuteronomy 8:5 says, *"As a man chastens his son, so the Lord your God chastens you."*

How does a father chasten his son? He punishes him, disciplines him and directs him along the right path. That's what the Lord does with us. If I discipline my own life then maybe the Lord will have to discipline me a little bit less. He won't have to smack me to keep me on the straight and narrow path, if I attempt to do it on my own. He's more pleased when I do it than if He has to correct me.

When your child does something correctly that you've disciplined them in the past about and they do it of their own will and own accord, it's pleasing to you as a parent.

That's the way it is with God. God doesn't want to punish, correct and discipline us but He will for our good. He's far more pleased, however, if we take the initiative of learning His statutes and covenant and then discipline ourselves.

If discipline then is training, instruction and exercise, what training do you need in your marriage? Think about yourself not your spouse. What area do you need more discipline in? What areas need training, instruction and exercise? What steps do you need to take to put that discipline into practice on a day-to-day basis? Maybe it's being kinder to your spouse. Maybe you have to develop an exercise, a daily discipline to be kinder to your spouse, like forcing yourself to have a kind greeting when you walk through the door in the evening.

Even though it may be a ritual at first, it creates a habit, which eventually becomes second nature. Then you can learn to enjoy that habit. Once you get past the instruction, exercise and discipline, then you get to the third step of a great marriage, which is delight. That's how you can have a delightful marriage.

Desire - Discipline - Delight

If you have a desire that you turn into a discipline it then becomes a delight. A delight is defined by Webster as a high degree of pleasure or enjoyment, a joy, a rapture, something that gives you great pleasure. Is your marriage relationship rapture? Psalms 37:4 says, *"Delight yourself also in the Lord, and He shall give you the desires of your heart."*

We go back to desire. Delight comes about when desire becomes discipline then discipline becomes delight. But our first delight has to be in the Lord, and then He'll give us the desires of our heart.

The Lord gave me the desire of my heart to be in full time ministry as I delighted myself in Him. I knew I was called to the ministry but not sure of what area. So I kept busy in a full time job and ministry on the side and God put it on Pastor Barnett's heart to ask me to join the pastoral staff.

The Lord gave me the desire of my heart, which was full time ministry, as opposed to secular work because I delighted myself in Him.

For a couple of years, Molly and I were having trouble conceiving a child. Then we just gave up and said we're just going to delight ourselves in God. No sooner than we did that, we conceived a child. We delighted ourselves in the Lord and He gave us the desires of our heart.

I had a desire to reach the people of Africa who were dying of AIDS. Through a miraculous set of circumstances the Lord sent me on a trip where 1 was able to minister for ten days in crusades. We saw 1,400 people with AIDS come to the Lord. Again, I delighted myself in the Lord and He gave me the desires of my heart.

I found a high degree of pleasure in my time with the Lord. I found pleasure in His Word, then He gave me the desires of my heart.

But first I had to know what my desire was, check it and make sure it lined up with the Word of God.

Then I had to discipline myself daily to live in the disciplines I needed to build my life up to move forward day by day.

Isaiah 58:13-14 says, *"If you turn away your foot from the Sabbath, from doing your pleasure on My holy day and call the Sabbath a delight, the holy day of the Lord honorable, and shall honor Him, not doing your own ways, nor finding your own pleasure, nor speaking your own words, then you shall delight yourself in the Lord; and I will cause you to ride on the high hills of the earth, and feed you with the heritage of Jacob your father. The mouth of the Lord has spoken."*

That's pretty strong when God ends a passage of scripture with *"The mouth of the Lord has spoken"*.

Many people don't know how to delight themselves in the Lord so He will give them the desires of their heart.

Here's step one. It says, "then you shall delight yourself in the Lord." You shall delight yourself in the Lord after you've made sure the Sabbath day is holy. After you've rested in the Lord. After you've taken that day not to do your own will and bidding, but to rest in the Lord and to see the Lord at work in your life.

We are to take one day out of seven and dedicate it fully to the Lord. That should be a delight. We should look forward to being in God's house on Sunday, rather than dreading it.

Normally children will do a little less than their parents did. If your children see you approaching church on Sunday grudgingly, what do you think they will do? They'll approach it more grudgingly.

Is Sunday a delight in your life? Is it a day you use to get your own agenda done or is it a day you use to rest and delight yourself in the Lord? The Lord will help you get more of your own agenda done in the remaining six days of the week if you use Sunday to rest in Him.

If we will just take time for God, turning away from doing our pleasure on God's Holy day, and call the Sabbath a delight, then we'll be delighting ourselves in the Lord and He'll cause us to ride on the high hills of the earth.

MANY PEOPLE DON'T KNOW HOW TO DELIGHT THEMSELVES IN THE LORD SO HE WILL GIVE THEM THE DESIRES OF THEIR HEART

If my desire for my marriage is right and lines up with the Word of God then He's going to have me ride on those high hills and really be blessed. God will give you that desire if you are focused on the right desire. Again, what is the right desire?

It is to delight yourself in the Lord and He'll give you the desires of your heart. The first desire is to love the Lord your God with all your heart, soul, strength and mind.

Haggai 2:5-7 puts it this way, *"According to the word that I covenanted with you when you came out of Egypt, so My Spirit remains among you; do not fear! For thus says the Lord of Hosts; 'Once more (it is a little while) I will shake heaven and earth, the sea and dry land; and I will shake all nations, and they shall come to the Desire of All Nations, and I will fill this temple with glory, says the Lord of hosts."*

What is God saying there? He says I'll shake all nations and they shall come to Jesus.

Our innermost desire is to come to Jesus. That's the desire God has created within us. We don't even know what our other desires should be and how they should line up with the Word of God unless we desire Jesus first.

It's interesting that Jesus is cited as "savior" about 37 times in the New Testament. He's cited as "Lord" more than 600 times.

Do you know Him as Lord? Do you have that desire so that every time you take a step He'll direct it? Do you desire to know Him that way, to know all about Him and all about His person?

You can know if you've taken and made His Sabbath holy; if you've delighted yourself in Him, He'll give you the desires of your heart and then you can ride on the high hills of the earth. That's His promise to you.

When you put these three steps into practice in your marriage, it can truly be a delightful marriage.

You begin with desire. Consider today what the desire is for your marriage. Look at the discipline it will take to accomplish your desire. Maybe it will be a discipline in your prayer life or Word life.

Most people desire to pray, but you must discipline yourself to pray even when you don't feel like praying. If not, you never get to the point where prayer becomes a delight. Many want revelation from the Word of God, to get fresh knowledge and deep insight into the Word, but unless you discipline yourself to study and ask the Holy Spirit to reveal it to you, you'll never get to the point where reading the Word of God becomes a delight. It will just be drudgery. You've got to enact that discipline. You've got to move from desire to discipline for it to be a delight.

The same holds true for your marriage. If you've got a desire for a great marriage, look at the areas you need to discipline. What do you need to do to be a better spouse?

IF YOU HAVE A DESIRE FOR A GREAT MARRIAGE, LOOK AT THE AREAS YOU NEED TO DISCIPLINE YOURSELF IN.

How are you going to take the training and put it into exercise so it becomes a discipline? When it becomes a discipline then it becomes a delight.

Is it a delight to take out the garbage? It should be. I'm thankful every time I take out the garbage that we live in a home and have garbage. Rather than having garbage thrown on my doorstep I have garbage to throw out. I'm thankful for that. You need to learn to make the disciplines of life a delight. Then as you delight yourself in the Lord constantly, He'll give you the desires of your heart.

Ask God to help you take these simple principles and apply them to your life.

Be honest with yourselves in asking what is the desire for your marriage.

What is the discipline you need? Do you delight yourselves in the Lord? Do you allow your spouse to be imperfect?

Discuss these things with your spouse.

PART THREE
THE PASSION OF MARRIAGE

GIVING SEX!

Sex is a very vital subject. The church for many centuries has re-pressed teaching about what proper sex is. It's a vital part of your relation-ship. A marriage is the three elements of a person coming together spirit, mind and body. Those are the three elements we are made up of.

These elements are interdependent in marriage, none is totally with-out the other.

We've heard the concept of marriage where the sexual relationship is the two coming together in body. But that's wrong.

The sexual relationship for a couple is the two coming together in body, mind and spirit.

It is the one activity where simultaneously, two people can give of each other to each other with every element of their being. When that activity is not in the proper Biblical perspective, then a great blessing is missed, even tragedy can result.

Sex is sacred. It is one of God's greatest gifts to us.

He created the female human species with a clitoris — the only spe-cies with an organ expressly designed for pleasure. That's not a mistake.

God did that on purpose. It's something very special.

If God is the Creator, and He created us in His image and the sexual relationship is that which creates life, then it's pretty special to Him. But we try to keep our sexual relationship separate from our spirituality. That's an offense to God.

Sex is holy, sacred and so very profound. In Genesis 4:1 when Adam knew Eve, the word "know" is the Hebrew word yahdah. It means intimate knowledge. It's the same word used for the tree of knowledge of good and evil in the garden. God uses the same word to describe the tree of knowledge of good and evil and the relationship between a husband and wife when they come together physically. It's that intimate knowledge.

The wonderful aspects of the sexual relationship - two people coming together in body, mind and spirit simultaneously — should be one of the highlights of our life. It's a forerunner or foretaste of how wonderful it will be when we're with God in heaven.

One of the interesting but sad facts about sexual relationships today is that people in the church have gotten their information from the wrong sources. People in the church have learned their information from outside the church. I believe a lot of the responsibility for the sexual immorality in the United States today lies with the church for not teaching openly about the wonderful gift of God that sex is.

SEX IS HOLY, SACRED AND SO VERY PROFOUND.

If people don't learn in a church setting where will they get their information? They'll get it from their peers, the world and worldly books, not recognizing the importance and spiritual significance of how it's set up for us to enjoy as part of God's grace to us.

How often have we heard of sex as something you do or something you have? A lot of couples think sex is something they do or have. Those are very worldly concepts. They are not God's concepts at all.

If sex is something you do, then your attitude is one of performance. You'll seek confirmation in your spouse, whether your performance was adequate or whether their performance was adequate. If sex is something you do then you're concerned about the act rather than the spirit.

If sex is something you have, then it's not performance but it's possession. It's something you lust over. If you have sex, it's possession.

The very way we refer to sex can indicate our attitude toward our sexual relationship. Sex isn't something a Christian couple should do or have. *Sex is something Christian couples should give.*

Since it is a gift of God, then we need to make it a giving relationship. Freely we have received then freely we give. If we look at our sexual relationship with our spouse as a giving relationship, then we remove the fleshly lustful element and it's easier to make it part of your spiritual relationship.

Pray Before Sex

Once it becomes part of your spiritual relationship, you begin to pray before sex. You can ask God to bless it and make it a part of your holy union. If you pray and ask

God to make it a giving experience rather than a taking experience, you improve the purity of your motive in the sexual relationship. Lust always takes, but love always gives.

The physical thrill of sex can create a subliminal bondage in your mind to where some people feel they have a need for sex.

That is simply not true. You have a want for sex.

LUST ALWAYS TAKES, LOVE ALWAYS GIVES!

Some men say, "I need sex regularly."

No, they want sex regularly.

"Well, uh, you don't understand what happens to me physiologically, if I don't have sex for a certain period of time." God understands that.

He created a release for it. He created nocturnal emissions for men who have not had sex for a while.

God created a way to deal with that. The question is whether your spirit is in control and you view that as part of your spirit man or whether you're utilizing it totally as a bodily function and simply gratifying the senses.

As a Christian, we must crucify the flesh and build the spirit. If you build the spirit man then you'll enjoy the fleshly part as a benefit from God rather than be driven by the fleshly part as an obsession of your mind.

God wants us to view sex as holy and sacred. Hebrews 13:4 says, that marriage is honorable among all and the marriage bed is undefiled. The term in the Greek for marriage bed is the word koite from which we get co-itus, the very act of intercourse. The act of intercourse should be undefiled. It's pure, holy and sacred.

If you're not having holy sex, than you're not having sex at all. All you're having is some physical release.

You're not making love; you're making sex. If you have holy sex then you're making love with your spouse. But if you don't have holy sex than you're only making sex, not making love.

Dare to Care

Many men think their sexual desire is so important that it drives much of what they do. Men do receive a lot of their identity through the sexual relationship. Men are driven by their sexual identity and the sense of respect and admiration they receive from their spouse.

Women are driven by a sense of affection, care and security. Women get a lot of their sense of identity through their maternal nature - the ability to give out and care.

Why is it that women perform most of the ministry in Christian circles today? Because part of the way God created them, their very nature, is the ability to care.

In Dr. Cho's church in Seoul, Korea, he has 50,000 deacons and deaconesses. Forty-seven thousand of them are women, in a society where women are not honored. It's simply because women, by their very nature, want to care.

Giving Sex!

Men, by their very nature, don't care. They want to be gratified. That's not necessarily bad, but it's important to understand that God created us differently as men and as women.

Not A Need, But A Want

Men need to come to grips with the fact that sex isn't something you need but it's something you want. It's not wrong to want sex. In fact, you should desire a wonderful marital sexual relationship.

When you start to look at sex as holy then you can come to the point where sex becomes spiritual warfare. Sex is one of the highest forms of spiritual warfare.

I Corinthians 7:2-5: *"But since there is so much immorality, each man should have his own wife, and each woman her own husband.*

The husband should fulfill his marital duty to his wife, and likewise the wife to her husband.

The wife's body does not belong to her alone but also to her husband. In the same way, the husband's body does not belong to him alone but also to his wife.

Do not deprive each other except by mutual consent and for a time, so that you may devote yourselves to prayer. Then come together again so that Satan will not tempt you because of your lack of self-control."

That's amazing! God is saying that we are supposed to engage in regular marital sexual relations so that Satan won't be able to tempt us.

Why? Because it is the one effort where we come together in body, mind and spirit. There is a unifying factor that's developed in a marriage with regular relations.

What is regular? It depends. For some couples, it's once a day, for others once a week and for others once a month. Whatever is by mutual agreement, with consent, each time.

Some people use sex to manipulate their spouse. Defrauding your spouse occurs when you keep sex from them as another means or another tool. At that point you're engaging in fraud.

God's plan is that you don't use that element of your relationship for any form of manipulation.

Yet I counsel couples all the time that use this form of manipulation, where the sexual relationship is viewed as a reward. It isn't a reward. It's a requirement. God says engage in sex regularly. The people who live longest on the earth engage in regular marital sex.

Studies were conducted in Soviet Georgia (now an independent state) where the oldest people on earth were found. Doctors wanted to know why they lived so long. They began to study the sexual habits of these people. Upon interviewing these people, some as old as 110 or 113 years old, they discovered that the common characterisitic among them was that they engaged in regular marital relations.

I don't believe there are only physical benefits but there are also spiritual benefits - the two becoming one in body, mind and spirit of having that intimate expression of love. That's what sex is - an intimate expression of love, not just a physical release, a great time and a good feeling.

SEX IS ONE OF THE HIGHEST FORMS OF SPIRITUAL WARFARE

You won't be able to adequately and intimately express your love to your spouse in your sexual relationship unless you view it as a gift from God that you are to give to your spouse (the gift of God that He's given to you).

In other words, if sex is a gift that God has given you and you are to give it to your spouse who is also a gift from God that He's given you, then that's very special. If you view it that way, then it's not something that's a demand on your part.

I'm amazed at how many Christian couples have their sexual relationship all messed up. They use fantasy for arousal and foreign objects to tickle and provide pleasure for themselves. That's not Biblical.

Any time you introduce a foreign object you're dividing that unity that God has created for you. He's given you every tool you need to give pleasure to your spouse. You don't need to play mind games or use fantasy to become aroused in your bedroom.

Fantasy is just another term for lust. It's just another way to deal with lust in your life.

If you're engaged in sex that isn't holy then you're in sin. It's one of the primary areas where Satan attacks marriages to divide people.

Let's view sex as spiritual warfare — the Word of God does. *"Do not deprive each other... so that Satan will not tempt you because of your lack of self-control."* I don't believe that means Satan will necessarily tempt you physically with lust after another, but he will tempt you in dividing you in your relationship and creating sin if you're not engaged in regular marital sex because you're depriving or defrauding one another. The only time to not have regular marital relations the Bible says is *"with consent for a time that you may give yourselves to fasting and prayer."*

That's what I call a sexual fast. I've recommended to many couples who've had their sexual relationship out of balance that they set a time and engage in a sexual fast. They determine a length of time where they won't engage in sexual relations but they will learn to touch each other in love. As body, soul and spirit we have different forms of relationship. Our soul relationship is our friendship one to another. Our spirit relationship is fellowship with one another and with God. The body relationship is intimate love. The sexual relationship is a part of those relationships.

Each element affects the other. If you don't have the physical love-making then your friendship won't be the same. If your friendship isn't the same, you won't have any intimate touch outside the bedroom, especially if your sexual relationship is wrong.

One way you can check yourself is to reflect on your physical touch outside the bedroom. Do you hold hands, hold shoulders, snuggle up, or touch your spouse affectionately? If not, then maybe there's something wrong in the body relationship.

Recently, I was speaking to a man who told me that while he was sitting on the couch with his wife, crossing their legs one over the other, it led to sexual arousal. I told him that perhaps sex was an idol in his life. There's nothing wrong with that being arousing, but if it's only that way, (if it doesn't have a sense of intimacy and a sense of love) then your friendship relationship is out of line. Your fellowship relationship (your spirit in tune with God's Spirit) may be out of line because your flesh is overriding your spirit. Your body is emphasized before spirit. Your spirit should be sensitive to the fact that you're in a moment of unity with your spouse. That should be your primary response.

If there's physical arousal afterward, it's a benefit of the spiritual relationship being in order. We have to recognize that we are body, soul and spirit. Unless we keep putting the spirit man first we'll be out of line and Satan will be able to tempt us in different ways.

Sex is Important to God

The sexual relationship is so important to God that the only man (other than Abraham) that God said He credited righteousness to for all generations was a man who consistently stood up against sexual immorality. His name was Phinehas. He was the grandson of Aaron and a great high priest.

In Numbers 25 he put a spear through an Israeli man fornicating with a Moabite woman in the tent of meeting in the temple: sexual immorality in the church!

Because no one stood up against it, God had sent a plague that killed 23,000 Jews in one day. This is also referred to in I Corinthians 10:8 when it says to refrain from sexual immorality lest 23,000 of you die in one day die.

Sexual purity is such a vital topic to God that to the man who stood up against sexual immorality in His house, God credited righteousness for all generations. That's a powerful promise.

Look at it in terms of the Old Covenant and the New Covenant.

In the Old Covenant, God's promise to bring His people out of bondage, the last area of sin He dealt with in His people to clean them up before they crossed the River Jordan into the Promised Land was the area of sexual immorality.

God permitted a plague that killed 23,000 in one day, but when the man of God stood up against sexual immorality that plague was stopped - ice cold!

And God credited to him righteousness for all generations!

It's amazing that you don't hear much preached about Phinehas. He's referred to in several different books in the Bible and God said *"to him is credited righteousness for all generations."*

The church has repressed teaching about sexuality, because Satan has established a grand scheme of deception concerning this area of our lives in which we can be conformed to the image of the Creator.

An early New Testament church leader, Origen, castrated himself in front of his congregation. How about that for a different Sunday morning worship service?

Martin Luther forbade sex on Wednesday, Thursday, Friday and Saturday, until he got married. Then he changed his doctrine.

Throughout history the church has had a distorted view of sex.

Why? Because it's one of the primary areas of Satan's attack. We're created in God's image and sex is an area where we create life. It should be a spiritual area, so Satan is going to attack it.

Since it's one of our most pleasurable experiences in both the physical and spiritual realms, he wants to hinder that. So, he's made it an area of such bondage.

We're a nation of people in bondage in the area of sexuality. We're a nation of church people who have a wrong attitude about sex because we haven't studied the scriptures to see what God says about it.

Hot Sex Tips

Here are some other areas that will help you:

When it comes to warming up sexually, most men are a microwave and most women are a crock pot. It's not always true, but in the many cases it is true. It can be freeing to understand that.

But if sex is a spiritual event that you approach with prayer, then God will create a balance for both of you. If your sexual lives are out of balance, then maybe you're not making it a spiritual event first. Maybe you don't understand the importance of marital relations as spiritual warfare.

It's one of the few places where God says, "do this or else you're letting Satan mess with you, he will tempt you." God's call to be engaged in spiritual warfare against Satan through regular marital relations encourages marital sex.

Some of us need to learn to communicate during marital sex. It's not just an event. It's a holy and sacred time. You need to laugh and enjoy each other's presence. You need to be able to enjoy God's presence.

PEOPLE WHO DO NOT KNOW GOD CANNOT HAVE GREAT SEX

By praying beforehand you make it a triune (a three in one) experience. It's then husband, wife and Holy Spirit. If the Holy Spirit isn't in your bedroom, you are missing out on one of the greatest experiences of life.

Many Christian couples have sex no differently than worldly couples. They come together in body and mind but the spiritual aspect isn't there. First Corinthians tells us that people who are not spiritual don't understand spiritual things.

People in the world can't have great sex. People who do not know God cannot have great sex. The fact that they can is a lie. They can have great physical release but that's not great sex. Great sex is body, mind and spirit. If the Spirit's not in your bedroom then you're missing out.

I believe many demons have the task of messing with people in their sexuality because it's one of our greatest creative functions in life.

Much sexual sin, however, is the result of unbridled, unrestrained flesh and not always demonic activity. Satan doesn't have to defeat those that defeat themselves by living undisciplined lives and not crucifying their flesh.

Created in the image of the Creator, we create life. We also create pleasure for one another as the symbol of unity in marriage.

It's the symbol of two coming together in total unity. If two are coming together in total unity in body, mind and spirit simultaneously then that couple has a prayer life.

Couples usually have a prayer life together if their bedroom and sexual life are holy. If they pray before their sexual relationship, it's likely they pray for other things too.

Satan wants to interrupt a couple who have the power of agreement in prayer and then have the physical unity to back it up so that nothing else can tempt them. *"Do not deprive each other... so that Satan will not tempt you because of your lack of self-control."*

If you're madly in love with your spouse and having wonderful, spiritual holy sex, it will be hard for someone to interrupt that marriage, whether it be with a physical lust, a transfer of affection, an attraction or anything else. If your marriage bed is undefiled, if your intercourse is holy and sacred, it will be difficult for anyone else to interrupt your marriage. Satan knows that.

Many have never looked at sex this way. Look at these things and study them together with your spouse. If you look at them alone, Satan will tempt you with being judgmental toward your spouse and their part of the sexual relationship. When you study these things together you can let the Spirit guide you and together you can receive from them.

Several years ago I taught a six-part series that some have said is the most graphic teaching on various aspects of sex in marriage they've ever heard. I'm thankful we recorded it, because I was a little uncomfortable teaching it. God has used that audio series, *Sex Is War!* throughout America to restore health in the lives of countless couples. It is a recommended resource for those needing to open up with each other about their sexual relationship.

In this day, the church that will be strong is the church that is sexually pure. Often, when we've seen a great falling away in a church, some form of sexual immorality has been involved.

Every time we see a church that lacks power we can see there are people who are out of covenant relationship in that church. If you've made a

135

covenant with God, a promise that will not be broken, about your spouse, then you will lose power if you break that covenant. It doesn't matter how you break it.

Jesus said in Matthew 5:28 that if you lust after another man's wife with your eyes it's the same as committing adultery. If you're having holy, sacred sex then no one else will tempt you. That's what God says: "*Do not deprive each other... so that Satan will not tempt you because of your lack of self-control.*"

Many need to repent for not having holy sex — for taking that precious gift of God and reducing it to an animal act. Animals cannot come together in body, mind and spirit.

The Holy Spirit of God is grieved looking at two people in their bedroom having an animal act. He says, "I want to bless you. Won't you let me be a part of that? Let me make it complete." Maybe you've never really thought of it that way. Pause for a minute and think about your sexual relationship. Maybe you're the one who has deprived your spouse of regular marital sex, or used it as a tool in your marriage.

Maybe you've never viewed it as your spiritual responsibility in marriage, or as spiritual warfare and Satan is messing with you in other parts of your life because your marriage bed is defiled and not holy.

Consider the holiness of your marriage bed. Talk openly with your spouse about the holiness of sex in your home. *The act that creates both new life and intense intimacy is holy.*

LOVE WHEN IT HURTS

Have you ever been hurt by your spouse — even small hurts? We're all hurt at some point in the marriage relationship; unfortunately that's part of our imperfect nature. Today, multitudes in our society need to know how to love when it hurts.

Hurt comes in a variety of forms, from mild disappointment to violent physical destruction, and everything in between.

In order to understand how to love when it hurts, we've got to understand our relationship with God as it applies to our worship. We worship God because we love Him. Once I choose to love God, I give up my right to worship Him my way.

Yet churches are full of those who come into God's presence and think they know what to expect from God.

They want to worship God on their terms. They want the same kind of feeling they had last time they worshiped Him. They want worship on their terms.

When we really worship God, however, and really love Him it's not on our terms. By the very commitment of saying we come to worship God, we give up our right to worship Him our way. Abraham was the best example of that. God asked Abraham to sacrifice his son. He asked him to lay him on the altar and actually kill him. That was God's worship plan for Abraham. What a bizarre worship plan!

It was not what he expected. It was against God's normal plan, that is, against the way God normally moved in Abraham's life.

Why? It was against what God taught.

God, just a few chapters earlier, spoke displeasure at the pagan practices of sacrificing their own children to their gods. Then God tells Abraham to take his only son, the gift of God he waited almost 100 years to get, and place him on the altar and sacrifice him.

Abraham's answer to Him is really incredible. As crazy as it seems, Abraham understood that sacrifice was a necessary part of worshipping God. And obedience was greater than even the sacrifice itself.

FAITH ACTS IN LOVE AND WORSHIP

Genesis 22:5: *"And Abraham said to his young men, 'Stay here with the donkey, the lad and I will go yonder and worship, and we will come back to you.'*

He told the men he was taking his son to be sacrificed on the altar and he said, 'The lad and I will go yonder, and worship.'" He understood the sacrifice of his son as an act of worship.

When he got to that place he knew they would come back. He knew God would provide a way of escape from the very point of pain in his life if he was obedient to the sacrifice that God asked him to make. He told the men, "we will come back to you." He was saying Isaac and I will come back to you, but we're going up yonder and worship.

He knew if he obeyed God in that manner and sacrificed his son, that he would return with his son. God would provide a way of escape.

The New Testament says Abraham offered (past tense) Isaac, because his act of obedience was the sacrifice that was necessary. It was the offering that was necessary.

Faith acts in love and worship. When faith acts in love and worship it's found in our obedience and willingness to obey God. That's where we learn the real meaning of worship. So the real meaning of the word worship is to totally give over my will to the will of God.

When we sing praises to God and then God's presence comes in, our real act of worship is not just a tingly feeling. It is giving over our will to the will of God. It's saying, "I love you God with all my heart. No matter what occurs in my life, I love you with all my heart."

When your spouse hurts you are you willing to worship God? That's a big question today.

Are you willing to give over your will totally to the will of God, even when your spouse hurts you deeply? As I thought about this, I thought about many couples I've ministered to over the last few years.

ARE YOU WILLING TO GIVE OVER YOUR WILL TO THE WILL OF GOD, EVEN WHEN YOUR SPOUSE HURTS YOU DEEPLY?

There are some dramatic examples, yet these principles are true in every case, even in a small hurt. The principle of loving when it hurts holds true. The principle of obedience to God's command of loving one another as Christ has loved you holds true in every single circumstance, even in the dramatic examples.

When we're hurt deeply, the tendency is to go inside ourself, to isolate ourself. But that's exactly the time we need to look for support and go outside of ourself.

When you are hurt deeply, for example, if your spouse sins against you in a dramatic way, then what the enemy does is to battle for your mind — for you to get alone, not share that hurt with anybody, and say, "Woe is me... I've been hurt... How horrible it is for me."

But what you really need to do is to look outside to the Body of Christ and get support from someone in prayer. Get an outside perspective on the situation.

You'll never really get victory over your own pain if you look at it from your own circumstances. It's only when you remove yourself and look from the outside in that you get victory over your own pain. At that time you no longer have a victim mentality, but God equips you to respond in love. We all have to love.

Every one of us has a desire to love. Everyone must love. Spurgeon said that everyone will love something. They will love a dog or a bird but they will love something.

Everybody loves that way. You've heard stories of prisoners of war learning to love the rat in their cell or the spider on the wall. Everyone has in them a desire to love. We're built that way, and we will love something.

The most destructive form of love is loving ourselves only. When we love ourselves selfishly we will create pain for those

THE MOST DESTRUCTIVE FORM OF LOVE IS LOVING OURSELVES ONLY

around us. We won't be giving to our spouse, by loving ourself and putting our own desires and needs first. That's what causes pain.

Pain can be so deep when the object of our love hurts us. When our spouse hurts us it hurts deeply because they are the object of our love.

The tendency when we get hurt by our spouse is to say, "Why have you done this to me?" That is love from a selfish motive.

You shouldn't ignore the pain. The pain is real. You're hurt when your spouse sins against you. But what you have to do is try to remove yourself from your own selfish perspective and look at it from the outside.

A dramatic example of this is King David. After he was in adultery and murdered, he realizes that his sin is not against people as much as it is against God. This will help you deal with your spouse if your spouse hurts you.

In Psalm 51:4, David says, *"Against you, You only, have I sinned, and done this evil in Your sight. That You may be found just when You speak, and blameless when You judge."*

David's true repentance came when he recognized that his sin was not just against people, not just against Uriah when he committed adultery with his wife Bathsheba, but his sin was against God.

140

Love When It Hurts

If your spouse hurts you, you'll be able to deal with the pain better when you recognize the pain your spouse is causing you is not just against you. The fact that it's against you is totally secondary to the fact that it's a sin against God.

Then when you view your spouse as having sinned against God, you're able to use God's love, compassion and mercy to say, "Wow, that person is in a broken condition. That person is not in right standing with God. That person doesn't understand what's going on."

Self-Inflicted Wounding

Does that make it any less painful? No. But it helps put a perspective on it so that you can understand that person is in pain also. Then God can begin to work with us in the situation. I thought about a dramatic example of a couple where the husband was involved in adultery. He finally came to the realization that not only was he sinning against his spouse and not only was he sinning against God, but he was wounding himself as a result of that adultery.

Proverbs 6:32-33 says, *"Whoever commits adultery with a woman lacks understanding; he who does so destroys his own soul. Wounds and dishonor he will get."*

We don't understand the pain caused is not only against our spouse but inflicted on ourselves by our sin. If your spouse has hurt you, you must understand that when your spouse is inflicting pain on you, they are also inflicting pain on themselves. Look at it as God looks at it.

The spouse's offense is not just against you. But when your spouse offends you, that spouse's offense is against God and themselves as well as against you.

Now you're able to see a broader picture and to see the path of destruction Satan would like to bring into your marriage when your spouse sins against you, even if it's a small sin such as a sharp or terse word that hurts you.

It's Satan's plan not only for that spouse to hurt you, but also for them

141

to sin against God and to wound and dishonor themselves. When you see that you begin to understand you have to respond in love.

Otherwise your very Christianity is challenged. If your spouse hurts you and you do not respond in love, then maybe you'd better re-examine your walk with Jesus Christ. Maybe you'd better re-examine what your faith level is like, because it takes great faith to overcome pain.

But in essence, God is saying we have to decide in faith to love. I Corinthians 13 says, *"Love never fails."* It endures all. It bears all things, including all that pain your spouse may bring against you.

If you are truly in that marriage as a covenant relationship before God, then God will give you that agape love to bear all and to endure all. His promise is that His love in you will never fail. He promises that restoration and healing will occur.

If you decide in faith to love your spouse when they hurt you, then God will restore and heal. That's His promise. The key to God's restoration and healing however is that you get into His Word and are able to appropriate these promises for yourself.

God's Word reflects our lives to us. The Bible tells us that the Word of God acts as a mirror in our lives. One of the greatest aspects of hurt that happens to us when our spouse hurts us is that it breaks trust. Trust is constantly earned and built.

When hurt breaks trust, it is a deep hurt that creates insecurities, defensiveness, and suspicion. If your spouse has hurt you repeatedly then your insecurity, your defensiveness and your suspicions will tend to increase, especially for a woman. One of a woman's basic needs is security. If her husband hurts her, her insecurity is built and her defensiveness and suspicion toward him will increase.

How do we deal with broken trust that comes from pain? How do we overcome the insecurities, defensiveness and suspicions?

The truth that God revealed to me is that if we listen when we're hurt, God usually deals with us about us. He'll deal with me about me when I'm hurt.

God is dealing with us all of our lives. He's trying to grow us through-

142

out our lives. When we're hurt, if we don't listen to our pain but to the voice of God, He usually ministers to us about us.

In the example I cited of the man who committed adultery, the wife chose to not be bitter but to take responsibility. She evaluated whether something was wrong. Maybe he was not receiving enough love. She chose to seek God about her responsibility in this relationship. I'm not absolving him of his adultery. We know it's sin and God hates it. But this wife chose to look through her pain at what God was telling her through this. She accepted responsibility.

WHEN WE ARE HURT, IF WE DON'T LISTEN TO OUR PAIN BUT TO GOD INSTEAD, HE USUALLY MINISTERS TO US ABOUT IT

When we listen to God when we're hurt, He then exposes our own faults and shortcomings, thus keeping us humble and dependent upon Him. When you're hurt, you can see your shortcomings with a brokenness of heart that will keep you humble. That's why God loves a broken heart. The humility that comes out of that recognizes responsibility and leads to repentance.

One might think, "This seems backwards. Isn't the person who sins supposed to be the one to repent?" Yes, but you have no control over that.

You are not the Holy Spirit in your spouse's life. You cannot make your spouse repent. You can beg, scream and shout and force them to say, "I'm sorry" but that isn't going to create repentance in their heart. Repentance is an act of self-will before God.

When we're hurt, if we don't listen to our pain but to the voice of God, He usually ministers to us about it.

It's a change of thinking decided and acted upon by that person.

You do have control over your own repentance.

You'll say, "Well I'm not the one who sinned. I didn't create the hurt." But you still need to repent. Why? Because we each sin as part of our nature.

If you feel you have no need of repentance, maybe you're not aware of how God is speaking to you and refining you all the time.

We all have need for repentance all the time. But sometimes it's in those times of hurt that we come to that humble place before God where in our humility we recognize that we have a responsibility for what occurs in our relationship. Even if our spouse hurts us.

The spouse I was talking about recognized her responsibility. Maybe she didn't love her husband as much as he required. Perhaps her nagging and complaining made him more susceptible to the wiles and guiles of the enemy because she wasn't loving unconditionally at all times.

She recognized that if she didn't look through her pain at what God was speaking to her then she would be destroyed by that pain. Instead she rose above her circumstances. On a much smaller scale, every little pain our spouse inflicts on us does the same thing. Unless we look at what God is saying to us through that pain, we're going to allow that pain to embitter us and defeat our relationship. It will also build a wider and wider gap as opposed to building our relationship in Him.

Recognizing Responsibility Leads to Love

When we recognize the responsibility we need to take, then we come to a place where we can love in agape love, which is God's unconditional love flowing through us. We recognize the brokenness of the sinner. The person who hurt us has sinned. Then we can get to the place where, like David, we recognize what's going on.

In Psalm 25:16-18, he says to God, *"Turn Yourself to me, and have mercy on me, for I am desolate and afflicted. The troubles of my heart have enlarged; bring me out of my distresses! Look on my affliction and my pain, and forgive all my sins."*

Interesting: *"Look on my affliction and my pain, and forgive all my sins."* That refers to the affliction and pain David felt in remorse for his sins. But I also believe if you take it in the context of the psalms right before it, Psalm 23 and 24, David is really looking at the pain that's been inflicted upon him.

Love When It Hurts

He says look at my affliction and my pain and forgive me of my sins. Not only for the pain I have brought upon myself, not only the wounds and dishonor I have brought on myself but those pains and afflictions others have brought on me. They've helped me realize I've got responsibility for actions in my relationships that I need to repent of.

Then he says, *"Consider my enemies, for they are many; and they hate me with cruel hatred. Keep my soul, and deliver me; let me not be ashamed, for I put my trust in You. Let integrity and upright ness preserve me, for I wait for You."* Psalm 25:19-21

If you want God to deliver your spouse from an area of sin, to heal your relationship, to change your spouse from causing pain in the way they communicate to you or whatever it may be, then you have to wait in God.

GOD WANTS TO BUILD AN IDENTITY IN YOU THAT IS ROOTED IN YOUR RELATIONSHIP WITH HIM, NOT IN ANY HUMAN RELATIONSHIP

David says let my integrity and uprightness preserve me, for I wait in you. When major crises hit a couple, I want to reach out and say, "Hang in there. Hang in there. Let your integrity and uprightness preserve you. Don't get bitter and angry toward that person. Recognize their broken condition. And wait in the Lord and God will honor that agape love."

His promise is that agape love will never fail. Wait in that uprightness and integrity. Stand firm and allow God to take up the battle for you.

In I John 4 we are challenged that even in the midst of whatever occurs in life God tells us to love. It's quite a challenge.

I John 4:7-8, *"Beloved, let us love one another, for love is of God; and everyone who loves is born of God and knows God. He who does not love does not know God, for God is love."*

Apply that to your point of pain, especially when your spouse hurts you. He who does not love does not know God for God is love. That's exactly what the enemy wants when that pain comes in; he wants you to remove yourself from knowing God, rather than taking your pain to God and saying, "Okay, Lord, deal with me through this issue. How do you want me to rise above it in love?"

Instead, we look to our own pain and then we don't know God. But it's through knowing God we rise above those circumstances of pain and we can find comfort in Him. The responsibility to love breeds that repentance.

1 John 4:9-11 says, *"In this the love of God was manifested toward us, that God has sent His only begotten Son into the world, that we might live through Him. In this is love, not that we loved God, but that He loved us and sent His Son to be the propitiation for our sins. Beloved, if God so loved us, we also ought to love one another."*

This should remind us that God forgave us so we ought to love one another, even when we have been hurt.

We must forgive our spouse when our spouse hurts us. Our spouse is a part of us - the two have become one. We have to recognize that in the same way God in His mercy forgave us, we have to forgive our spouse. Then the Lord builds an identity in you that is rooted in your relationship with Him, not in any human relationship. That's the most powerful lesson you can learn from any pain in your marital relationship.

He wants to build an identity in you that is rooted in your relationship with Him, not in any human relationship. That's challenging because we really love to love in our marriage. That's important, but greater than that God wants you to love Him with all your heart.

Often we take that pain of hurt in our own relationship and rather than to look to our first relationship, the love of God in our lives, we dwell on our own pain.

Then we don't know God. We can't see God loving us. Unless we accept responsibility for sin in our life and repent and get away from our sin, we can't know God. We can't be one with Christ. It's only through oneness with Christ that you'll overcome the pain that your spouse creates.

Only through the love of God can you overcome by examining yourself and asking, "What area do I need to clean up? Am I bitter toward that person who caused me pain, even though I love him or her?"

You must remove that bitterness or otherwise Christ and you cannot be in unity.

I must separate myself from sin in my life. Then I can truly be one with Christ. I must be contrite and confess and ask God to forgive me of my sin or I cannot have that relationship with Him. Once you develop that relationship with Him, once you get to that place where you're in the love of God, you'll know God will give you the strength and patience to wait on God to work in your spouse's life.

You can only get that security if you and Christ are united and in agreement. That's why the enemy attacks us with pain because through the pain he wants us to be bitter, unforgiving, distant and isolated from others so that we don't look for support, prayer, strength and fellowship.

Alone, we wallow in our own pain and say, "Woe is me." We can't see God's hand at work. We can't even see that He's there for us, that He will give us the strength and patience to wait on Him to work even in your spouse's life.

Psalm 40:1 says, *"I waited patiently for the Lord; and He inclined to me, and heard my cry."* It didn't say I waited for the Lord. It says I waited patiently. You can wait, but often you might wait impatiently. When you are hurt by your spouse, wait patiently for the Lord to heal that hurt.

Impatiently, you might respond, "Well I'm hurting now," rather than responding patiently, "Okay God, I put this in your hands. I see that maybe my spouse has hurt me. I'm going to press into You. I'm going to accept responsibility for my own life. I'm going to love you closer and closer and wait patiently for You."

"And He inclined to me, and heard my cry. He also brought me up out of a horrible pit, out of the miry clay." Psalm 40 :1-2

Sometimes when there's dramatic hurt in your marriage it can be like miry clay or a horrible pit. You feel you're trapped. Maybe your spouse has a besetting sin, an ongoing type of sin, such as lying or lust, or some other repetitive sin pattern. You feel you're trapped in that miry clay.

But God says if you wait patiently for Me I'll incline to you. I'll hear your cry, deliver you and raise you up out of the miry clay. Then David says, *"And set my feet upon a rock, and establish my steps. He has put a new song in my mouth - Praise to our God; many will see it and fear, and will trust in the Lord."* Psalm 40:2-3

I thought of the previously mentioned couple. When he saw his wife's unconditional love and forgiveness and that she accepted responsibility for her actions in the relationship, he feared it just like David said, "Many will see it and fear, and will trust in the Lord."

He feared it and trusted in the Lord. He recognized that God was greater than anything he could do and he repented of his sin because he saw the unconditional love of his wife.

He was remorseful before, but he repented when he saw the unconditional love of his wife.

When you're in a point of pain, rather than get upset, dwell on the pain or even receive that pain and stay in it, say, "Lord, what are you dealing with me about through this. Why are you even permitting this pain in my life? You've got to show me something through this. Deal with me. Let me see what my responsibility in dealing with this pain is." Then you no longer have the decision to stay hurt. You're one with God. You're pressed in with Christ. You know God and you know His love so it's no longer your decision to stay hurt.

What do I mean by it is no longer your decision to stay hurt? Galatians 2:20-21 says, *"I have been crucified with Christ; it is no longer I who live, but Christ lives in me; and the life which I now live in the flesh I live by faith in the Son of God, who loved me and gave Himself for me. I do not set aside the grace of God; for if righteousness comes through the law, then Christ died in vain."*

He's saying that grace is greater than the law. There's a liberty that occurs. It's no longer me but Christ in me!

This verse reveals more than just the spiritual. Sometimes people think, "Well if I'm spiritual I'll just rise above that. But the scripture says, *"The life which I now live in the flesh I live by faith in the Son of God."*

Even though you might not feel spiritual at that moment, you're choosing to live by faith in God. When you live by faith in God, then you understand that you can rise above any point of pain, even in fleshly moments. God will quicken to you that He is love and that your relationship with Him is paramount.

Your relationship with Him is the thing He's trying to develop along with the reality that our marital relationship is founded in our relationship with Him. My relationship with Molly is rooted in my relationship with God, not in my relationship with her or in how we react or respond, but in my relationship with God.

If Christ lives in you then you can walk through even those things in the flesh, in compassion and mercy. You can learn to respond in compassion and mercy all the time. James 2:12,13 says, *"So speak and so do as those who will be judged by the law of liberty. For judgment is without mercy to the one who has shown no mercy."*

If you understand that, then you can live in Ephesians 4:32 when your spouse hurts you. It says, *"Be kind to one another, tenderhearted, forgiving one another, just as God in Christ forgave you."*

Jude 20 emphasizes the same principle that even when we're hurt, no matter what the situation we have to love. *"But you, beloved, building yourselves up on your most holy faith."*

Is God in Your Marriage?

HOW TO AVOID HARD TIMES

Colossians 3:12-13 says; *"Therefore, as the elect of God, holy and beloved, put on tender mercies, kindness, humility, meekness, long-suffering; bearing with one another, and forgiving one another, if anyone has a complaint against another, even as Christ forgave you, so you also must do."*

These are the characteristics that we put on.

How do you go through the hard times in your marriage? A prominent leader once intimated to me, "Stay close to God so you don't have to go through the hard times. I found myself getting closer to God during the hard times. But stay close to God so you don't have to go through so many hard times."

It's in the hard times that we press closer into God. But this man's words were very profound in my life: "Stay close to God so you don't have to go through so many hard times."

These verses in Colossians 3 tells us some of the characteristics we need to put on so that we're close to God. If we're close to God in those ways, we can avoid some of the hard times.

"Put on tender mercies." Sometimes I think we can be merciful without

being tender. We can be merciful to others out of obligation or out of the sense of the right thing to do.

Sometimes people say I'm tired of doing the right thing. I'm not experiencing the love of God in my life. Are you doing it tenderly? Maybe you're being merciful, but is it a tender mercy? We have to examine our heart.

Religious people often do the right thing but they don't do them spiritually. It takes a spirit in tune with God's Spirit to be merciful, tender. A lot of people can be merciful out of obligation or ritual. Some of the great homeless shelters of the world are merciful out of ritual but they don't have a spiritual affect because the mercy isn't tender.

"Put on kindness, humility, meekness and long suffering." While these are attributes of the Spirit, they are things we can put on.

We put on meekness which is a vertical relationship, understanding who we are with God. We put on longsuffering or self-control. We put on these things even though they are of the Holy Spirit. That does not mean we deny the fact that the Holy Spirit can sovereignly place those things in our lives.

RELIGIOUS PEOPLE OFTEN DO THE RIGHT THING BUT THEY DON'T DO IT SPIRITUALLY

But more importantly, God wants us to put these on in order to activate these attributes in our lives so the Holy Spirit can then enhance them and let the fruits of the Holy Spirit be made known.

In the past year would your relationship with your spouse have been better had you daily put on tender mercies, humility, meekness, longsuffering and kindness? The second part of the scripture means we are to be bearing with one another and forgiving one another.

Frequently when I conduct a marriage ceremony, in my prayer of benediction at the end I often say, "God let love be the language of this home. And let understanding and forgiveness be the dialects of that language."

We need to remind ourselves that understanding and forgiveness are the dialects of the language of love. In other words, they are slang, the language that is native. A dialect is a language that's native to an area. Obviously, New Yorkers speak differently than those from Oklahoma. In your home there's a dialect.

The language of love that's in your home is unique to your husband and wife relationship. And the dialects of that language of love are understanding and forgiveness. That's what this verse is referring to. It refers to bearing with one another and then forgiving one another.

Activate Understanding

If a marriage is going to realize God's benefits and stay close to God without having to go through the hard times, then it must activate understanding. It has to always be ready to speak forgiveness. Forgiveness is a vital aspect of realizing love.

As an example, let's say my spouse and I are having a crisis. I've worked at understanding why my spouse is having this crisis, why things are going wrong in my spouse's life. If I work at understanding that, then my spouse will feel my understanding and will be less likely to go into a downward spiral in the crisis, which means I won't have to forgive more and more.

Sometimes when someone steps into an area of sin or deception in their life and they're in a downward spiral, they will distance themselves further and further from their spouse. Especially if they feel that their spouse is not understanding of what they're going through. They then might spin further and further into that cycle of depression, sin or emotional distance in an attempt to avoid pain. But, if they're in that crisis and confusion and trauma sets in and they feel their spouse has understanding for them, then they will turn toward their spouse.

That's what we're supposed to do in our marriage. We're supposed to be an evidence of God's love one to another. That's why Romans 8 and Philippians 2 talk about preferring one another. As we prefer one another, our spouse receives our understanding of their condition and then they can thank God because the love of God is shed abroad in their life through their spouse. Their spouse has now become evidence of the gift of God in their life. At that point, it endears them toward the other and they say, "Hey, this person has understanding." And that's what we're drawn to.

If we activate understanding and forgiveness then the language of love in our home will communicate better because we'll understand the dialects. Sometimes we don't understand the dialect of our spouse when they're crying out for understanding or when they are testing the waters to see if there's forgiveness available.

If we don't pick up on the signal of our spouse placing their toe into the water to see if there's forgiveness, we can limit the ability of our spouse to confess sin and for healing to occur.

We have to be sensitive to those dialects of understanding and forgiveness.

After bearing with one another and forgiving one another it says, *"If anyone has a complaint against another, even as Christ forgave you, so you must do also."*

What a wonderful reminder of why forgiveness needs to operate in our lives as Christians. Even as Christ forgave you so also you must do. I believe if you dwell on that simple sentence, you can forgive anyone of just about anything.

Were you deserving of Christ's forgiveness? Not I.

When He showed His grace to me, I was not deserving. Were any of you deserving when Christ forgave you? No, of course not. None of us was deserving of God's grace when it came into our lives. But as Christ forgave us so also must we do.

The High Call of Marriage

To forgive as Christ forgave us is the high call of marriage. Constantly we're called to forgive in situations where we may feel justified, at that moment, to not have to forgive our spouse.

But that's when we must forgive. Just as Christ forgave so we must also do. Ask God to reveal to you how you can put on tender mercies, exemplify humility and kindness to your spouse.

"But above all these things put on love, which is the bond of perfection." Colossians 3:14

Above understanding and forgiveness we're to put on love.

Even in times when your spouse seems unlovable, put on love, in the same manner in which Christ put on love for you when you were unlovable. Just as He forgave you, so must you also forgive. That's what putting on love is all about. That's why we state that love is a decision not a feeling. There are moments of ecstasy and loveliness.

But that's not what love is. It's a decision where we put it on. We determine that we're going to love.

If you're putting on love all the time toward your spouse you would not raise your voice toward them.

If you're putting on love toward your spouse, you'd be more tolerant of their dream and vision as opposed to trying to express your own all the time.

> IF YOU ARE PUTTING ON LOVE TOWARD YOUR SPOUSE, YOU WOULD BE MORE UNDERSTANDING OF THEIR DREAMS AND VISIONS INSTEAD OF EXPRESSING YOUR OWN ALL THE TIME

We have to try to put on love. Love is not just something that happens in our lives. That's a twinkle, an attraction or infatuation, and sometimes when someone isn't receiving that understanding and forgiveness at home they open themselves to an infatuation or an attraction that would occur away from home. That's not love.

Love is a decision, a walk, and an energy that comes from God alone. That's why in order to put on love, we've got to stay close to God so that we don't go through the hard times.

You can't put on love without God.

I John 4 says; *"God is love."* And I Corinthians 13 says; *"Love never fails. It bears all and endures all things."*

I'm challenging you to examine this passage and ask yourself if you are putting on love or are you falling back into the daily doldrums of living "my own life".

If you stay close to God you'll think of things eternal, not just selfish pursuits for the present. You'll have a value for other souls and for heaven in your life. If you think about temporal things you'll think of your own personal needs, and you will revert to selfishness.

Most of the time what we think are needs are really wants disguised as needs. We've had things we thought were a need taken from us and we survived without it.

Have you ever had your car in the repair shop for more than one day? You thought you needed that car, but really it was a want. You survived without it.

God wants you to have a vehicle if it helps in your lifestyle and helps in producing income for your family, but it's a desire.

Let's not confuse our wants with our needs. There are plenty of people who survive without a vehicle. It's not a need.

A need is something that's vital to survival. That's why many men think they have a sexual need. But they don't. They have a want, a desire. It happens to be a strong desire, an important desire, but it's not a need. If you get to the point where you think it's a need, then you elevate it to a position in your mind where it's such a vital aspect of your relationship that it overcomes putting on love. That's where sexual idolatry comes in.

Anytime we take a need and develop it to a place where it's higher than where God intended it to be in our lives, that's a form of idolatry.

According to Colossians 3, what are our needs? Our spiritual needs are that we put on tender mercies, kindness, humility and self-control. We need those things in order to stay close to God so that we can: 1) speak the language of love, 2) have the dialects of understanding and forgiveness activated in our lives, and 3) receive God as love and put on love in bearing with one another in our own lives.

If you do that you'll see that's a tough road, a lot to do, a tall order. We need to examine ourselves one day at a time against what the scripture says we should be and do. My challenge to you is to get back to basics in your marriage and in your relationship, and put on love.

In order to do that you've got to stay close to God and activate your daily prayer life. Husband, it's up to you as the spiritual leader in the home, according to I Corinthians 14, to instruct your wife about spiritual matters, to lead your wife in prayer. If you don't have a set time to daily agree with your wife in prayer, you're missing a blessing. Therefore, you can't expect to stay close to God to help you through the hard times.

Back to Basics

There's a responsibility God calls a man to as spiritual instructor of the home. Maybe you feel that your wife knows more of the Word, she's more spiritual, and knows how to pray better than you do. I'm advocating a simple prayer of agreement. It could be just 30 seconds of agreeing in the name of Jesus. You must have your own personal prayer life, but God wants you to have that agreement with your spouse also. One sets one thousand to flight, and two sets ten thousand to flight. Return back to the basics of agreeing together as a couple.

Return to the basics of having the Word of God in your life. Many men are discovering the power of the Word of God for the first time in their lives. The church needs strong men. Where there are strong men there are fruitful women. God's Word places a lot of the responsibility on men.

We need to become men of the Word, not men of theory, worldly principles, psychological principles, or school knowledge, but men of the Word of God. If we have men of the Word then we'll have men like Jesus.

What woman wouldn't want to have a man like Jesus? We need that more than ever. We've got to get back to those basics.

Wives, you've got to resist the temptation for rebellion in your home. There's a spirit of Jezebel across this country that is making women rebellious toward their home. It's activating the natural woman who is rebellious toward her husband. Most women are rebellious and most men are lazy in their natural condition.

You've got to resist that desire. In an attempt to stay close to God we must rise above the natural and become supernatural. The word super in the Latin means to be above. We try to rise above the natural. That's what supernatural means. But we can only do that with God's help. If we rise above the natural then ladies, you won't be rebellious, but you'll understand the joy of fulfilling your role in Christ. Men if you rise above the natural then you won't be in the natural condition of laziness.

What man wouldn't love to be sitting on the couch with the remote and their wife feeding them grapes? But the natural man has to work. The supernatural man rises above and begins to enjoy his work, being thankful for his health and his ability to provide for his family. He appreciates his position, which is putting on love.

In order to put on love you've got to find out what love really is. It's not a feeling or emotion. It's God!

The same way we received God into our hearts by making a decision to do so, is the same way we receive the love of God into our life and pour it out upon our spouse. Receive, pour out, put on love and avoid the hard times.

THE MYSTERY OF ONE FLESH

Matthew 7:9-12: *"Oh what man is there among you who, if his son asks for bread, will give him a stone? Or if he asks for a fish, will he give him a serpent? If you then, being evil, know how to give good gifts to your children, how much more will your Father who is in heaven give good things to those who ask Him! Therefore, whatever you want men to do to you, do also to them, for this is the Law and the Prophets."*

This is one of the most challenging passages of scripture. Yet it is used in secular organizations and it is used in corporations throughout the world. People refer to it as "The Golden Rule."

"Do unto others as you would have them do unto you." I had heard that principle before I became a Christian. Those raised in church probably heard this passage of scripture preached a lot.

Who would give someone a stone if they asked for bread?

Can you imagine reaching into a breadbasket expecting a roll, you peel back the napkin and without looking you reach in, take a bite of one and crack a tooth?

What man, if asked for bread would give a man a stone? Or if asked for fish, give him a serpent?

Is God in Your Marriage?

Seattle, Washington is known for its fish market, a huge fish market with huge tables of fish — all the big fish are there. You call out what type of fish you want. A worker picks it up and he heaves it across to you. You're supposed to catch the fish with the plastic gloves they provide you; it's an experience.

What man, if asked for a fish, would give a serpent?

Can you image if somebody were at that fish market and he said, "Hey, let me have that big bay salmon over there" and the worker reaches out, picks up a huge snake and throws it at him.

If We Would Only Ask More

That's what Jesus is saying, "This is ridiculous."

Yet you don't believe in prayer. For he started out that passage saying, "ask and you shall receive" and he's saying "Do you think that if you ask of your Father, the Father who is all merciful, all good, all powerful that if you ask of Him bread, that he'll give you a stone?"

The problem is that we are not asking. We're not asking in faith because we don't believe that Father God is good enough. We wonder if we ask for a fish are we going to get a snake thrown at us. We wonder if we reach in the breadbasket if we are going to get a stone.

If we really believe that our Father in heaven is good, and that He's good all the time, then we would ask Him and know that if we ask Him for bread, that He would not want us to crack a tooth. We would know that. Yet, in the final verse of this passage, when Jesus is instructing them about faith and receiving from God, He indicates that, for all things, in all things, through all things, at all times, whatever you want men to do to you, you should do that to them.

In faith, believing that whatsoever ye shall ask ye shall receive, I want to call you to raise your level of faith for your marriage. Whatsoever you ask, you shall receive. But part of the key there, is placing yourself in the position of offering to your spouse that whatsoever you would have your spouse do unto you, are you doing it unto them?

160

I'm tired of husbands and wives blaming each other. Every time you point a finger, there's three fingers pointed straight back at you. Every time you operate in judgment, God says in Matthew 7:2, Whatsoever judgment you measure out, so shall it he measured unto you.

When we point to blame, the Spirit of God comes to us and says, "What about your life? How do you respond? Why are you putting all of the burden on your spouse when I'm interested in your heart? Leave their heart to me. That's my business," says the Spirit of the Lord.

"What about your heart? I'm looking right in there right now. Where is your heart? Next time you open your mouth to make your spouse want to change, consider your heart!"

If I believe that God is good and He's good all the time, then I should have faith to ask and that the change I desire, should occur through my intercession for my spouse.

Change will not occur when, in my human imperfection, I'm trying to inflict change on my spouse, but only as the Holy Spirit would come down into my spouse's heart and make that change. That's faith. It's not faith to go hide for three hours and search out all of the rebuke, reproof and correction scriptures to have a shopping list of admonitions when your spouse comes through the door.

Before I became a Christian, I had never heard many of the Christian speak terms such as "admonitions, exhortations, etc." People just don't walk around using that language every day, so be real with your spouse. If you've got an admonition, tell them "Hey, I believe I have a warning from the Lord." But if you proudly state that you have an admonition, then people may start to resent your spirituality.

We must be sincere with our spouse and we've got to be able to operate in that "whatever you want them to do to you, you do to them" mentality.

Take that further, into your family. What's the relationship with your parents or your in-laws like? Some are pleading for that unconditional love from their parents. Are you operating in it? God places the burden right here. Right here with us and that's where it has to lie. But this is a principle that holds us back from unity in marriage. As long as we don't operate with our spouse in "whatever we want them to do to us, if we're not doing that to them", then we're dividing the unity and we're not fulfilling the purpose of marriage.

In Genesis 2:24, God says:

"Therefore, a man shall leave his father and mother, and shall cleave unto his wife; and they shall be one flesh." KJV

When you don't do to others as you would have them do unto you, then you risk the chance of becoming hypocritical and even Pharisaical.

In fact, the Pharisees always used controversial issues in their relationships in an attempt to trip up Jesus. They did that in John 8, with Jesus' response to the adulterous woman. And they do it in Matthew 19 with the controversial issue of divorce.

Talking to different preachers around the country on the phone, I'm often asked, "Where do you stand on divorce?" That's how the Pharisees came to Jesus, "Where do you stand on divorce?"

"And great multitudes followed Him; and He healed them there."

Notice that oftentimes it's at the point of healing that religious hypocrisy manifests.

"The Pharisees also came unto Him, tempting Him and saying unto Him, "Is it lawful for a man to put away his wife for every cause?" and He answered and said unto them, "Have ye not read, that He which made them at the beginning made them male and female?" Matthew 19:2-4 KJV

That's what I feel like when pastors around the country ask, "Where do you stand on divorce?"

Have ye not read that God hates divorce in Malachi 2:16 because he seeks godly offspring? Of course, we hate divorce.

Have you not read that the only unpardonable sin is the blasphemy of the Holy Spirit? And yet so many ministers want to treat divorce like an unpardonable sin.

Do you want to heal those people who have gone through rifts, or are you like the Pharisees trying to use that as an issue to judge them.

Then you can feel better about your own rebuking, reproofing and correcting? Should we operate in love? Should we do unto others, as we would have them do unto us?

What if your spouse was an adulterer and a fornicator and ran off with everybody in town and then decided to divorce even though you wanted to stand for the marriage? What then? Would you do unto others, as you would have them do unto you? What if you were in that situation?

Would you want somebody to say, "Well, you're divorced, you're not worthy."

What is God's attitude? The whole Bible is a book about people's lives who were not worthy to serve God. But when they got into His presence, all of a sudden they realized that it was not themselves that made them qualified anyway! Hallelujah!

Yes, God hates divorce and I hate divorce with all my heart. But if you've been through a divorce, I'm going to love you with all my heart.

The attitudes of some of the churches in America today create a Pharisaical, hypocritical division that stops our people from walking in unconditional love.

"Have ye not read, that He which made them at the beginning made them male and female, and said, For this cause shall a man leave father and mother and shall cleave to his wife; and the twain shall be one flesh?" Matthew 19:4-5 KJV

This verse of scripture is not only repeated here from Genesis 2:24, it also appears in Ephesians 5.

Why is the one-flesh relationship so vital? Because if we can't operate in unity that way, if we can't operate in "whatsoever we would have them do unto us do we unto them" in our marriage, how are we going to do it as a church?

How are we, as the people of God, going to show the unity of the Holy Spirit to a lost and dying world if we can't even do it in our own homes?

Jesus repeated in verse six: *"wherefore they are no more twain, but one flesh."*

He wanted to emphasize that. *"What therefore God has joined together, let no man put asunder."*

"For our comely parts have no need but God hath tempered the body

together, having given more abundant honor to that part which lacked." I Corinthians 12:24 KJV

God gives more abundant honor to the part of the body that lacks, and so should we. That's why Jesus said; *"The Spirit of the Lord is upon Me, because He hath anointed Me to preach the gospel to the poor, He has sent Me to heal the brokenhearted, to proclaim liberty to the captives and recovery of sight to the blind, to set at liberty those who are oppressed."* Luke 4:18 KJV

Do you want to be conformed to the image of God? Do you want to take on the character likeness of Jesus Christ? Well, then you'd better give more abundant honor to that one who's weaker!

Some fingers are beginning to unfold, no more pointing nor the blame game. Put that hand behind your back, tear up that shopping list of offenses, and throw it away.

There should be no schism in the body, but that the members should have the same care for one another.

What is a schism? It's a division. Schism is a fissure in the earth. It's where the ground has moved because the foundation has been unstable, the earth has cracked open. Left unchecked, uncared for, that schism can become a rift, and that schism can become a canyon of division that you cannot cross.

God desires that there be no schism in the body. We have to treat our spouse with more abundant honor even if we view them as lacking in the things of God. We're to treat them with abundant honor.

"Now ye are the body of Christ and members in particular." I Corinthians 12:27 KJV Let's take that to our marriage. If you are the body of Christ and members in particular, then each one of you is a member. Each one of you is a part, both you and your spouse are part of that unity and unless, together, you two can become one flesh, then the body is lacking.

Our good friend Dan McLennan hooked his wedding ring on a piece of machinery on a truck, and it ripped his finger off. He was dismembered. He lost a member of his body. A photograph of Dan's hand in the hand of his wife, Barb, is part of some of our ministry materials. It's the only photo they have of his finger, and it's from their wedding pictures. Even though he doesn't have that finger there, because of the unity in their marriage, God has used the picture of their two wedding rings together.

No matter what you have gone through, maybe you've been dismembered spiritually, maybe you've lost a piece of yourself, a piece of that one flesh; rather than let it be destruction in your life, you can turn it around and use it for God's glory

Are all spiritual spouses intercessors? Or are maybe some just worshippers? We've got to accept our spouses for where they are.

Maybe you are gifted in a prophetic ire with a hatred for sin but your spouse is motivated by mercy or compassion. Ye are members in particular. Accept each other as they are; don't try to inflict your spiritual gifting on your spouse. Go to God and let Him make you in His fullness so that you can be that best member in particular that you are supposed to be. Otherwise, the two cannot be one flesh. You'll miss it.

The Best Marriages Come from Incompatibility

In our premarital ministry, I often tell people, "Incompatibility is grounds for a great marriage." It sure is.

The best marriages I know are people who are totally incompatible who have learned to accept each other's differences and grow from them and learn tolerance and forgiveness for each other and for others as well as a result. God honors that, because forgiveness begins in acceptance.

Incompatibility can help you grow. You don't want to be married to somebody just like you. Let me prove it to you. Do you want to go to bed and make love to somebody just like you? No!

We want something different, something wondrous, something to explore, something to thank God for! We want another member in particular so that together we can become one flesh and give glory to God the Father.

"Husbands love your wives, even as Christ also loved the church, and gave Himself for it; that he might sanctify and cleanse it with the washing of water by the Word, that He might present it to Himself a glorious church,

not having spot, or wrinkle, or any such thing, but that it should be holy and without blemish." Ephesians 5:25-27 KJV

If you were out working on the car and you came in to eat a meal, would you wash every finger but one? Would you leave your index finger greasy and dirty? Of course not. You need to undergo a total washing by the water of the Word. We as husbands are called to make sure that our spouses are undergoing the washing by the water of the Word because we'll have to give an account to our Father in heaven as to how we present our wives. Did we do our best to wash, to scrub, to encourage, to clean and to present that spouse as glorious before the Lord?

What is your wife's spiritual condition and how much of it is dependent upon you as part of that one-flesh relationship being the member in particular where you are the right hand that needs to wash the left.

"So ought men to love their wives as their own bodies. He that loveth his wife, loveth himself" Ephesians 5:28 KJV

Paul knew that men are vain. He knew that men love their bodies. Some guys are overweight and they'll do a little flex so that their fatty pecs move. It's just fat wiggling, but they think they're all bulked up. Men love their bodies.

Men, in the same way that you would wash that dirty finger after having worked on the car, that's how much you're supposed to wash your wife. If you see her discouraged, bring her an encouraging word from the Word of God. Help her to undergo the washing by the water of the Word.

Stop blaming and stop pointing those other fingers.

"For no man ever yet hated his own flesh, but nourisheth and cherisheth it, even as the Lord the church. For we are members of His body, of His flesh and of His bones." Ephesians 5:29-30 KJV

It's very interesting that he says, *"For we are members of His body; His flesh, His bones."*

Imagine how Eve felt when all of a sudden she looked up and there was Adam in all his perfection, in his wondrous beauty. He had not yet fallen. He was conformed in the image and likeness of God and she looks up and he looks at her and he says, "Behold, woman. Now this is bone of my bones and flesh of my flesh." She probably couldn't wait to become one flesh!

She looked at Adam as if to say, "Yes, he has received me. Yes, he has declared me to be one with him."

That's the marital relationship. That's the relationship of Jesus and the body of Christ, that when we in our marriages as husband and wife declare our love for another, God is pleased.

Just like when Stephen, in the midst of being stoned, praised and worshiped the Lord. It says that Jesus stood up off of His seat at the right hand of the Father and said, "There's one of mine. Bone of my bone and flesh of my flesh." Just when we declare our love for our spouse, when we encourage them in the word, when we have a family altar and have a time of devotional prayer together, Jesus says, "Bone of my bone and flesh of my flesh."

It's time to undergo the washing by the water of the Word.

It's time to repair schisms; it's time to put divisions aside. It's time to repent. It's time to repent of even being judgmental and of pointing fingers. You may need to make a determination that the only time you open your hand will be to intertwine your fingers with your spouse. You'll not lift a pointed finger towards them. The only time you'll extend that index finger towards them is to have that touch together so that the two can become one flesh.

In closing, Paul declares, *"For this cause shall a man leave his father and mother, and shall be joined unto his wife, and the two shall be one flesh. This is a great mystery, but I speak concerning Christ and the church. Nevertheless, let every one of you in particular so love his wife even as himself and the wife see that she reverence her husband."* Ephesians 5:31-33 KJV

Remember, early on in this book, the challenge was issued: ***every Christian marriage ought to aspire to be the physical manifestation of the invisible reality of Christ and His bride, the church.***

Hopefully, you now view your marriage as the covenant God wants it to be, and have a vision to continue to grow in that direction.

Declare Your Marriage As Covenant

More than 75 leading marriage and family ministries have come together to be a part of the Covenant Marriage Movement, asking couples throughout the world to affirm their marriage as a covenant by agreeing and expressing the following to each other:

Believing that marriage is a covenant intended by God to be a lifelong, fruitful relationship between a man and a woman, we vow to God, each other, our families and our community to remain steadfast in unconditional love, reconciliation and sexual purity while purposefully growing in our covenant marriage relationship.

If you agree with that powerful statement that tens of thousands of couples all over have signed to signify their dedication to God's principles in marriage, take a moment to look your spouse in the eyes and exchange those words.

When you do, call our national office
toll-free at
1-888-262-NAME
or email us at
info@nameonline.net.

We would like to mail to you, free of charge, an attractive copy of the statement that you can frame and confidently display in your home, letting everyone know that indeed your marriage is a covenant subject to the promises of God.

Is God in Your Marriage?

If you have enjoyed this book, you'll love Dr. Leo's new book

Men Are From Dirt, Women Are From Men

This exciting book helps couples enjoy discovering their differences, with proven principles to enhance your marrige. Here's what a few leaders are saying about this fun read:

"As Men Are from Dirt, Women Are from Men takes you on the glorious journey of learning to understand your differences, it doesn't stop there. The seven proven and practical principles of learning to enjoy our differences as men and women after understanding them will certainly increase marital satisfaction for many couples. I hope you are one of them. Do yourself a favor; don't read this book alone. Read this with each other, and perhaps even to each other, so that you can maximize the benefits of discussing the journey of understanding your differences, while learning to enjoy and relish them on a daily basis."

Dr. Gary Smalley
Author, The DNA of Relationships

"Can you imagine what a God-given infusion of humility and biblical purpose would do for your marriage? Well, that's just what Leo intends to give you in this terrific book. Don't miss out on his passionate message. It just may revolutionize your relationship."

Drs. Les and Leslie Parrott,
Authors, Love Talk

"Dr. Leo Godzich has tremendous insight into the God-ordained differences between men and women. This book should bring a lot of clarity and healing to couples everywhere."

Dr. Tim Clinton, President
AACC, American Association of Christian Counselors

"In today's confusion concerning what marriage is, who qualifies and what each person's role is, it's good news to see God's standard of righteousness being proclaimed in print. Leo brings his teaching directly from the Word of God with a refreshing prespective. This book should be a part of every pastor's library and should be recommended by pastors to their congregations as required reading prior to a marriage counseling appointment."

Dr. Denny and Sandy Nissley
Christ in Action Ministries

Is God in Your Marriage?

THE THREE-FOLD MISSION OF NAME

ONE
TO CALL CHURCHES AND INDIVIDUAL COUPLES
BACK TO A BIBLICALLY-BASED,
CHRIST-CENTERED,
AND HOLY SPIRIT-EMPOWERED
PERSPECTIVE ON MARRIAGE.

TWO
TO NETWORK COUPLES
AND MARRIAGE MINISTRIES.

THREE
TO SPEAK WITH A RIGHTEOUS VOICE
CONCERNING MARRIAGE AND FAMILY ISSUES
IN THE PUBLIC FORUMS.

FOR MORE INFORMATION ABOUT NAME CENTERS AND THE
MANY ASPECTS OF NAME'S MINISTRY AROUND THE WORLD:
1-888-262-NAME
(602) 404-2600 PO BOX 71100 PHOENIX, AZ, 85050
OR EMAIL:
INFO@NAMEONLINE.NET

Is God in Your Marriage?

Is God in Your Marriage?

Is God in Your Marriage?

Is God in Your Marriage?

For further information about

NAME

THE NATIONAL ASSOCIATION OF MARRIAGE ENHANCEMENT

VISIT

WWW.NAMEONLINE.NET

OR CALL

1-888-262-NAME (6263)